KOVIASHUVIK

A time and place of joy

KOVIASHUVIK
A *time and place of joy*

Sam Wright

Sierra Club Books ∗ *San Francisco*

The Sierra Club, founded in 1892 by John Muir, has devoted itself to the study and protection of the earth's scenic and ecological resources—mountains, wetlands, woodlands, wild shores and rivers, deserts and plains. The publishing program of the Sierra Club offers books to the public as a nonprofit educational service in the hope that they may enlarge the public's understanding of the Club's basic concerns. The point of view expressed in each book, however, does not necessarily represent that of the Club. The Sierra Club has some sixty chapters coast to coast, in Canada, Hawaii, and Alaska. For information about how you may participate in its programs to preserve wilderness and the quality of life, please address inquiries to Sierra Club, 730 Polk Street, San Francisco, CA 94109.

Library of Congress Cataloging-in-Publication Data
Wright, Sam.
  Koviashuvik : a time and place of joy / by Sam Wright.
    p. cm.
  ISBN 0-87156-688-5
  1. Eskimos—Alaska—Brooks Range. 2. Indians of North America—Alaska—Brooks Range. I. Title.
E99.E7W9 1989
128'.4—dc19   88-31121
                                                        CIP

Production by Eileen Max
Book design by Abigail Johnston
Printed in the United States of America
10 9 8 7 6 5 4 3 2 1

Contents

Introduction *1*

1 Koviashuvik *3*

2 To Build a
  Log Cabin *14*

3 A Metagraph *19*

4 Being There *24*

5 The Great
  Blue Range *35*

6 Visit to America *51*

7 Haul Road
  Hard Hat *70*

8 Caribou *87*

9 Where is Truth? *98*

10 Itigak *111*

11 Voice from
   the Wilderness *124*

12 Transformation *134*

13 On They Went *143*

14 Tree Planting *149*

15 Pipe Dream *160*

16 Bless the Indians *164*

17 Koviashuktok *185*

18 Phalaropes *198*

19 Faith of
   Adventure *205*

Postscript *213*

KOVIASHUVIK
A time and place of joy

Introduction

How we know what we know is an exploration in which everyone is engaged in one way or another.

One of the most frequently asked questions among children is, "How do you know?"

And, among children, the most frequent answer is, "Because."

"Because why?"

"Just because!"

*   *   *

The question is the same after the years turn us into so-called adults. Although the question has been named as a branch of philosophy called epistemology (the study of how we know what we know), the question is still the same. So is the answer.

*   *   *

Anyway, this book is an adventure; not only in the wilderness north of the Arctic Circle in Alaska, which my wife Billie and I call home, but in the exploration of that first question, "How do you know?"

*   *   *

This book is, "Because."

To some this book may appear to be about theology. But knowing nothing about God, I am writing about epistemology.

I can write about epistemology because I have been given a proper degree in divinity and spent seven years as a professor in a graduate theological seminary.

As a professor in a theological seminary, because I knew nothing about God, I taught epistemology.

Before I taught epistemology, I taught biology in a university where I knew nothing about God. I still don't. I don't think anybody does.

This book is about a way of seeing on a journey I am taking with everyone else. And though our trails are different, we journey together from before time to we know not where it will end.

*   *   *

The question is where to begin? For in the beginning there was no beginning, even though Lao Tzu said a journey of a thousand miles begins with one step.

So, step with me into our log cabin, one hundred miles north of the Arctic Circle in Alaska at four o'clock one April morning . . .

1
Koviashuvik
Time and place of joy

I was sound asleep but must have sensed the grizzly bear at the door of the cabin.

When he raked the door with his claws, shoving it open, I jumped out of bed hollering at him and grabbed the rifle where it hung from a roof log. In one flow of motion I removed the scope covers, threw a cartridge into the breech while shoving my feet into boots beside our bunk.

It seemed like one flow of motion because I was outside in the snow and had fired a shot at his brown bulk as it disappeared in a flurry of white, kicked up as he galloped away through the spruce trees.

Stepping back into the cabin, my wife, Billie, stood just inside the door with the other 30-06 rifle held ready for action. Facing me, she stood with the other rifle pointed at my stomach. Actually, against my stomach, with her finger on the trigger and there we were.

There we were, and it was funny that we stood half dressed at four-thirty in the morning holding loaded rifles while the great bear was still loping off through the drifts.

It wasn't really funny because, a few days before, the bear had smashed in the windows and torn up the inside of our cabin while we were away. He would be back.

*　　*　　*

He came back when we were away in Seattle.

We were away in Seattle, Washington because Billie's book *Four Seasons North* was to receive an award from the Northwest Booksellers Association as the best non-fiction for the year. Billie could not receive the award because she was sick with the flu. It was funny that Billie could not get out of bed to receive the award after traveling all the way to Seattle. But it wasn't really funny, as it was not really funny that the bear got away. But it really was funny, our standing there facing each other with loaded guns. This was interesting because people everywhere who like each other but have a grizzly bear to deal with often find themselves facing each other with loaded guns.

*　　*　　*

We flew to Seattle so Billie could receive the award, but not just to receive the award, because we wanted to visit the British Museum and see London while the bear was in hibernation.

From Koviashuvik, it costs as much to fly to Seattle as to go on to London. And since this seemed the best time to go to London, if we were going to visit the British Museum, we flew to Seattle so Billie could receive the award so we could go to London.

Anyway, Billie was sick with the flu in Seattle and then I was sick with the flu in Seattle. In a hotel in Seattle we were sick for a week. In Seattle, on the eleventh floor with a black and white television set, we were sick and it rained.

*   *   *

When we were sick in Seattle we thought about London and the British Museum, but mostly we thought about Alaska and Koviashuvik and when the bear would come out of hibernation and how, if you are sick, it is better to be sick at home. Home is where you want to be when you are sick. So we went home.

Later we went to London and the British Museum which I tell about later.

This time we were sick and went home.

*   *   *

We were still sick when the bush pilot flew us over the high peaks, and the ski plane spewed out snow on the lake ice, but we were home.

The sun was shining and wolf tracks were on the trail as we pulled our supplies up the slope to our cabin. The mountains stood against the sky and the spruce trees were dark against the snow and, although the bear had come out of hibernation while we were gone and had smashed out the windows and made a shambles of our cabin, we were home.

I tacked plastic over the windows and we cleaned up the mess the bear had made. We took our supplies out of the cache and, with a hot fire in the Yukon stove, made chocolate and warmed our feet in blankets and went to bed because we were sick.

We were happy, even though we were sick, because we were home. Home is where we are, not where we dwell. When we are where we are it is home.

We are home at Koviashuvik in Alaska, but nearly everyone who lives in Alaska, except some native people, are not really at home in Alaska because they are going to live somewhere else some day. Yes, they are going to live somewhere else, like nearly everyone in America is going to live somehwere else or die somewhere else.

It is interesting that Koviashuvik is not somewhere else, or else we are already somewhere else which is home.

*   *   *

This is what I learned from the Eskimos.

Things are brought into being by speaking of them. Even if they were already there, they do not really exist in the way they exist when we are there or speak of them. They are no longer what they were before we were there or before we spoke of them.

There is no verb "to be" in Eskimo but everything that is said is a form of to be. We call where we live an Eskimo word, loosely translated as time-and-place-of-joy-in-the-present-moment, which did not exist when we first came to Alaska. Now it does. Every time we say it does. It is Koviashuvik.

Koviashuvik did not exist when we first came to Alaska because Koviashuvik is what we call where we live in the wilderness. We did not live here then, but it was here before we were here, but not really here, because we had not lived here or called it Koviashuvik.

Alaska was here before we came and it was called Alaska, and the Eskimos lived in Anaktuvuk Pass in the center of the Brooks Range and I had read how they hunted caribou, but I did not really know how they lived because I had not been here, so I came.

I came to Alaska because I had not been here. I came because I read how Robert Marshall had planted spruce seeds north of timber line in the nineteen-thirties before he died in the nineteen-thirties. They named the Bob Marshall Wilderness in Montana after him because he was dead. They name things after you when you are dead so you can exist after you are dead.

I wanted to know if Bob Marshall's seeds had grown and how the Eskimos lived in the Brooks Range before they began to live like everybody else in America lives.

*　　*　　*

Now I know. I was really looking for Koviashuvik, which did not exist. But it did exist, at least the idea did, even if it was not what was there before we were there.

*　　*　　*

Koviashuvik is not what it was when we first moved into the wilderness of the Brooks Range just before freeze-up. We did not know what to expect because we had never spent a winter alone in the Arctic. We thought we knew what to expect but there is a difference between knowing and knowing. Yes, there is a difference between knowing that the temperature will drop to sixty degrees below zero on the Fahrenheit scale, and knowing that there will be no direct sunlight for nearly three months, and knowing there is no way to call out, and knowing a steady fire is necessary in the Yukon stove to keep a 12 by 12 foot log cabin warm. This we knew, but we did not know how good it was the way we know now, which is why we call it Koviashuvik.

*　　*　　*

Now listen to this.

Billie had never been in the wilderness before the summer we visited the Eskimo Village in Anaktuvuk Pass and hiked the range to plant seedlings in Bob Marshall's plot on Barrenland Creek to test his theory of the movement of white spruce north of timber line. We planted one hundred four-year-old white spruce seedlings in his plot, in the plot where his seeds had not grown.

Yes, in 1968 we planted one hundred four-year-old white spruce seedlings where, thirty years before, Bob Marshall had planted seeds which had not grown.

This is also why we came to Alaska but not why we

stayed in Alaska or moved into the wilderness of the Brooks Range. We stayed because our adopted Eskimo grandmother said, "You do not know how Eskimo live unless you live like Eskimo early days ago, alone, in the wilderness."

We know now. We know.

We live in the wilderness because here we found Koviashuvik, which is not just a place but a way of life, which has chosen us as we chose it.

Yes, the way chose us like the bear chose us.

                    *   *   *

We called our grizzly bear the phantom because a phantom is apparent yet has no substantial existence.

Our bear did exist, however. Oh yes, our grizzly bear existed! For over two years the phantom existed at Koviashuvik. He was first apparent one spring when he tore up our winter cabin two miles from where we had moved into our summer camp.

On the shore of the lake where we spend the summer, like the Eskimos used to spend the summer at their fish camp on the lake, we built our summer cabin. The bear came to the shore of the lake and ate moose meat hanging outside the cabin and looked in the window where we were sleeping.

We did not know he was looking in the window because we were asleep. But the meat was gone when we awoke and his tracks were outside the window. We were joyful because he did not smash through the window into our eight by ten foot cabin like he did in our winter cabin five times one summer.

Five times he raided our winter cabin that summer and I slept in the cache with a rifle and put out bait and followed his trail until it was lost. Since the bear was not seen, we called him the phantom because a phantom is apparent but has no substantial existence. Jean Paul

Sartre said existence precedes essence, but he did not know our bear.

As I said, one night I fired a bullet at him, when Billie and I faced each other with loaded guns, and his claw marks on the door today make him apparent with no substantial existence. He was apparent like the Presidents of the United States were apparent in the Watergate and Iran-Contra affairs or apparent like the impact of the trans-Alaska pipeline project on the wilderness.

*   *   *

Anyway, when we came to Koviashuvik Billie had never lived in a wilderness, at least a natural wilderness, so when I shot our first caribou it was an experience for her. Yes it was.

She helped me dress it, which is really undressing it, by skinning, cleaning and quartering, which was really septering because it takes seven parts of a caribou to back-pack and hang, not including tongue, liver and other good things like the tundra in the stomach of the animal. The tundra in the stomach of a caribou is good to eat. It is.

Billie's meat had always come packaged from the market and although she knew someone must kill an animal and prepare the meat, it is one thing to think about something but another thing to know it.

*   *   *

I shot our first caribou on an island in the lake. We called it Caribou Island. We took our winter moose another year on Caribou Island and I snared a wolverine on the island where we pick cloudberries.

We still call it Caribou Island and it is.

*   *   *

To kill an animal for food is a sacred thing at Koviashuvik. Even picking berries is sacred, but not slapping mosquitos. No, it is hard to think that mosquitos and other biting insects have a value like ourselves but they do.

At Koviashuvik we had a visitor who liked to fish for the high-finned grayling which he caught with an artificial mosquito. He hated mosquitos and said fishing would be wonderful without mosquitos. He could have said that without mosquitos there would be no grayling.

The sacred emblem of the grayling fisherman should be the mosquito. This fisherman wore an elk's tooth. There are no elk in Alaska.

*   *   *

After we killed our first caribou we talked about life and death because philosophers and poets always talk about life and death in front of a Yukon stove. With tongue and testicles bubbling in the pot, we talked about life and death. Mostly we talked about life because death is only a part of life and life is what goes on. Entropy is on another scale.

Although death is real for an individual, death is life. When the fire dies we snuggle in our sleeping bag on the spruce pole bunk. In the dark we hold each other.

*   *   *

Then freeze-up comes.

Everything is silent.

Everything is silent except the lake which groans and cracks as the temperature drops below zero. With a great voice it cries and moans as it adjusts to the pressure of the freezing ice. It talks and we like to hear it alive as it freezes. Every autumn we like to hear the lake talk at freeze-up.

Then comes the sound of silence.

It is strange that silence is sound and cold is heat that is not there. Something is there because temperature is like the sound of silence. Even if you are deaf there is the sound of silence.

I have a friend who is blind and when I told him about

a golden poppy unfolding in the sun he said, "I see," even though he was born blind had said, "I see," not like those having eyes see not and having ears hear not.

In the wilderness we hear like my friend can see.

After several winters we went to Anchorage and San Francisco and Los Angeles and back to Anchorage. There we missed the sound of silence.

*   *   *

Winter north of the Arctic Circle is silence and cold and dark. But not really dark when the sky is coral and blue at midday, and stars come out bright in the early afternoon and the moon never sets when it is full, making long shadows on the snow from the base of every spruce tree.

It is cold at Koviashuvik. When it is sixty degrees below zero it is cold. We pull our wolverine ruffs around our faces and watch the claret and emerald curtains of the northern lights swirl from horizon to horizon.

In Anchorage we never saw such northern lights.

In the wilderness we can see.

Anyway, that first winter we did not know about the cold and it was interesting to put a bucket of snow in the water barrel which froze the water, instead of melting the snow, until all warmed up to freezing.

In the cold everything has to warm up to freezing. When we visited America everything needed to warm up to freezing.

*   *   *

We visited America when everything was freezing. To promote Billie's book, we lectured across the United States during the winter there was an oil and gasoline shortage.

In California people bought gasoline according to the number of their license plates and in New England they put blankets over doors of unused rooms and turned down the thermostats. It was cold and the atmosphere was cold toward the Arabs, like it was cold toward the Russians. Billie and I shivered in suburban homes.

Even after we spent a winter in Pleasant Valley, in the sunny mountains of Arizona, where we built a hogan of rocks and yellow pine, we shivered. We never shiver at Koviashuvik.

At Koviashuvik we are never cold.

*   *   *

We liked our first winter alone in the wilderness because everything was new and everything new is interesting. At Koviashuvik everything is always new. Even though it is old it is still new, like the one room log cabin in which we spent our first winter, built by George the Greek over sixty years ago on a slope five hundred feet above the lake.

We were told by Dishu, an old Eskimo, how a Greek built the cabin years before, and that his name was George. This was interesting because we never thought that Greeks called George built log cabins.

We never thought that we would live in the wilderness north of the Arctic Circle and build a log cabin. But we did and he did, and it is still interesting that his name was George.

When I asked if George had been a philosopher because he was a Greek, Dishu said he was a prospector.

"What is a philosopher?" the Eskimo asked. I said, "He is a seeker."

"Yes, that is what he was." Dishu said, "He was looking for gold, a prospector."

We moved into the old cabin high above the lake, built by the Greek prospector-philosopher, just before freeze-up.

*   *   *

In the 12-by-12 foot log cabin were a few supplies we needed which we did not bring in the cardboard box crammed behind the seat of the small bush plane. We did not need very much, like people do not need very much but think they need what they don't need.

The float plane taxied to the shore. While the pilot pumped water out of the leaking floats, we took out the seat so we could remove our crate of supplies.

Our pilot said, "See you in a month or so when I'm on skis," which was interesting because we had never seen a plane on skis, except in movies and television which are not real.

It was real on the shore when the plane disappeared over the mountain and we were alone. But we were not alone, for a loon called across the water and spruce trees were there and the moon was there and Billie and I were there as we climbed the hill to the cabin built by the seeker, George the Greek.

The cabin had been empty for six years after a prospector, who bought it from George the Greek, died leaving a few hand tools. There were cooking utensils behind a Yukon stove with a cracked top and rusted stove pipe. I patched the stove pipe with tin cans and we rechinked the logs and tacked cardboard from our box on the wall where other cardboard had been chewed by squirrels.

Billie arranged things where she wanted them and I brought water from the creek, hung the rifle from a beam and we were at home. We were at home as we have never been before. At home in the house that George built.

To everything there is a season and a time for every purpose under heaven.

ECCLESIASTES

2
To Build a Log Cabin
40 logs and 300 poles

The next spring we built a cabin on the shore of the lake. We built our cabin with old logs from dead trees as well as new ones from the living. I cut and trimmed the branches and adzed the bark from trees.

We stuffed moss between the logs so they would fit together. Even in the notches I chopped for the corners, moss filled the space between the logs. We did not call them trees when they were logs and when they were walls we did not call them logs.

We like the spruce trees when they are not logs and we admire the logs when they are walls in the spring sunshine. We like the walls with iridescent blowflies against the logs as the snow melts. As the snow melts we sit outside in the sunshine and eat sliced moose on sourdough bread. The first flies of spring hum in the sunshine and crawl on each other's backs to buzz new life on the golden logs that are the walls of our cabin.

At the shore we built our house with trees.

*   *   *

When I cut a tree there is always a young one growing near it. Always there is a younger one because we
like trees. When they are logs they are no longer trees.

The ax takes out a wedge as the tree becomes a log
for our cabin. I swing and the tree becomes our home
and our home defines a tree because we do not cut a
tree unless a new one is growing near it. Koviashuvik
is where we care for trees when they are not logs.

It takes forty logs to make the walls of our cabin. We
cut three hundred poles to hold the turf on the roof.
I wonder if I could build a cabin if I could not count. I
wonder.

*   *   *

We cut the tundra so we can put turf on the roof.
Under the tundra the ground is frozen. Under the tundra
is permafrost that will thaw when the tundra is not there.
Without tundra the permafrost becomes a pond.

Without tundra everything turns to muck in the Arctic. Tundra is the base in which everything lives so we
always leave some tundra when we cut it because it pro-
tects whatever is underneath. When it is on our roof we
are underneath.

*   *   *

Next we built a cache high above our heads. On four
posts we made a platform with poles. Tin cans were fitted
around the posts to keep out shrews. On the platform
we built a small cabin. We built our cache on the platform above the reach of wolves and bears and where we
thought a wolverine could not climb. But a wolverine
did. Three wolverines did.

Anyway, we built our cache to store flour, sugar and
our meat which is caribou and moose frozen in the
winter. In winter we always keep matches and extra

sleeping bags in the cache because fire is the most dangerous thing in the Arctic.

Fire is necessary to keep us warm and melt snow for water. Fire is necessary and we like the smell of spruce smoke when wood crackles and glows through the draft in the Yukon stove. Fire is still a dangerous thing.

A burning cabin in the wilderness is a dangerous thing. Even in Fairbanks or Las Vegas, fire is dangerous like an idea is a dangerous thing when it gets going. Ideas are necessary but an idea is a dangerous thing.

Utopia is an idea which is a dangerous thing, like the Kingdom of God or the American Dream, which can warm us in the cold or create a lynch mob.

Fire can burn down our cabin, so we keep sleeping bags and tools and matches in the cache.

*   *   *

We like running water at break-up, the sound of children out at recess. Voices are everywhere when the ice goes. A door of silence bursts open with bird songs and in the swollen creek rocks tumble and my ax is a beat to the harmony of white-crowned sparrows in the willows.

My saw joins the rhythm of sloshing water under the plunger in the tub of dirty clothes at break-up. At break-up a robin's song from the top of a spruce is a bursting of the door of silence and we sing with the plunger and the saw and the robin. At Koviashuvik we sing at break-up.

*   *   *

By the time birds arrive, stars have disappeared. When birds arrive in May it is no longer dark. It is night but no longer dark north of the Arctic Circle.

The three-foot-thick ice melts into candles with nineteen hours of sunshine. Gulls fly over the rotting ice and feed in the melt along the shore but no plane can land when the ice candles. When the ice candles it is not safe.

It is not safe while it looks safe as anywhere things

can look safe. But when the ice candles it will no longer support what it did before.

When the climate is changing everything looks the same but it is not safe. It is not safe in the world like it was.

*   *   *

I conducted a funeral service in Marin County, California for Hoagy Carmichael's sister because I had buried her husband the year before and he was a writer who served in the Lincoln Brigade in Spain. He had given up life and she killed herself because the world had changed for them. They felt it was no longer safe for them. But Hoagy Carmichael kept writing his songs during Hiroshima and Vietnam and the birds keep bringing their songs to Koviashuvik.

It is never safe when the ice candles. It is not like it was. But birds still sing everywhere in the world the birds sing.

*   *   *

Arctic terns arrive with the first open water along the shore. With deep forked tails and porcelain fluttering wings they hover over the shallows before dropping like rocks into the water. They plummet into the lake and rise with a small fish to swallow before flying with lazy strokes a few hundred feet before again hovering white against the sky.

The terns have flown eleven thousand miles. From Tierra Del Fuego, at the southern end of the earth, they have flown to nest at Koviashuvik. They follow the sun and we call them birds of light. They come after the ice candles and the dark has gone.

The dark has gone when the terns arrive.

We watched the birds arrive while we were building our cabin on the shore. We stopped to watch ducks glide in. In pairs they would plane to a stop on the water in the open leads. The ducks arrive in pairs in May, so do the sandpipers. Along the shore the high-finned grayling swim in pairs. Everywhere it is spring there are pairs when the sun shines.

*　　*　　*

We have orbited the sun nineteen times since we built our cabin on the shore. We have eaten eight moose, eleven caribou and one bear. We haven't counted snowshoe hares, ptarmigan, trout, pike, grayling or cloudberries. No, we haven't counted blueberries, lingonberries, or willow buds. We haven't counted everything.

It is strange that we count the number of miles to the end of the lake and how many days until the next airdrop and how many dollars to charter a bush plane and how many pounds a fish weighs and how many wolves are in a pack.

Everywhere people are counting how many days and how many dollars and how many pounds and how many miles as if everything is on account and everything is a number.

A blueberry is not a number and the gross national product is not really a number. Even if we think it is it is not.

*　　*　　*

A blueberry is a blueberry, not a number. Sunlight dancing on ceiling roof poles is not a number reflecting from the first touch of morning on the lake. Sunlight cannot be numbered the way we number everything. We do not really number everything but we would if we could. Yes, I think we would.

We built our cabin on the shore which was ten feet long and eight feet wide. With spruce poles I made a bed. With spruce poles I made tables and chairs. With spruce poles we made a home with spruce poles I did not count.

3
A Metagraph
Computing is not thinking

When I write I am more conscious than at any other time of things I feel and think and dimly perceive which I find impossible to put into words.

I am not peculiar in this. I am sure I am not peculiar. All of us feel that more goes on inside than we are able to tell others. At least I think all of us are aware of things we cannot express even to ourselves about the past and future or the meaning and importance of some event or our feeling about life itself.

*   *   *

We are aware. In some way we are aware that there is meaning within us and that our language is inadequate to express what this means to us, and so I say I can't tell you what this means to me in trying to tell you what it means to me.

When I say I shall miss you more than I can say I say more than I can say.

Anyway, I read between the lines when I read anything I try to read between the lines and write so there
is more than is said between the lines.

This is the way it is with writing even though we try
to be precise it is never possible. There is always more
between the lines.

*   *   *

This is the way it is with language whether it is written or said it is a way of speaking that says more than
is said. In the rhythm of our breathing and pulse of our
blood language comes from inside the body. It is the art
which comes from inside the body literally from inside.

Language is art because it uses all the same words the
same common words we use to complain about the
weather and talking to a neighbor and writing letters.
We fashion them with art when these puffs of meaningful sound are warmed by our heart and lungs and
shaped into moving utterance. When they are words on
paper they are art. Writing is an art.

I am writing at this moment about the Arctic and Sub-
Arctic of northern Alaska which is where we live in
America. But more than this we live within the world
as well as on this planet in a universe of ideas called
dreams and concepts because experiences are not places.
I am writing about Koviashuvik because Koviashuvik is
a uni-verse which is two Latin words and one truth is
not everyone's truth because the universe is not a place.
It is.

*   *   *

Anyway when Richard Nixon was president of the
United States a professor wrote me a letter and asked
why I wrote the way I did without proper punctuation
he said. I said people don't talk with the same punctua-

tion. The transcripts of the president's tapes were not punctuated like the speech writer's punctuation. I said I write with punctuation but it is my punctuation. He does read what I write the professor does. The president had his punctuation and deleted his expletives and so do I.

As I said, Koviashuvik is a way of seeing as well as a place. When Marshall McLuhan said the medium is the message he did not know the Eskimo language. He was talking about television which is punctuated with commercials and newscasts or is it the other way around?

I wonder what will happen to Eskimo when it is punctuated by professors. I hope not. But since I was a professor I know it will.

   * * *

So I wrote the professor period I said comma quotation marks My writing is metagraphical period close quotation then I defined my term colon quotation A metagraph is a written communication in which the structure of the communication is also relevant to the communication as a Whole in which the creation and interaction of ideas comma concepts and forms exemplify the process period paragraph quotation I am exploring the overlap between formal premises and actual behavior comma that is comma that area between abstract formal philosophical thought and the natural history of humans and other creatures in the context of their environment period I refer you to the writing of Alfred Habdank Skarbek Korzybski and Gregory Bateson's comma *Steps to an Ecology of Mind* comma Chandler Publishing Company comma 1972 period close quotes You will find it in paperback period then I hiked down the shore to catch a fish.

   * * *

In spring when the ice goes lake trout rise to the mouths of creeks to feed on grayling and other smaller fish which eat the larvae of mosquitos who need our blood to mature their eggs so larvae feed grayling and grayling feed the trout which feed us whose blood the mosquitos need even with repellent on us they get our blood.

Anyway, I caught a trout by casting an artificial lure made from a coffee can lid cut sausage shaped with hooks attached. At the edge of the deep water he grabbed the lure. I set the hook and there we were connected. Yes, we were connected by ten thousand years we were connected even by blood we were connected.

*   *   *

Ten thousand is a number.

When the fishhook was invented I wonder how much a ten pound lake trout tasted in numbers. What does a trout taste if it weighs twenty years old I wonder how many miles swum pounds eaten gallons gilled eggs spawned to arrive at a number for taste?

The French say there is no accounting for taste which makes a problem for the computer which thinks in numbers if it does think which it does if thinking is names and numbers.

Computing is thinking names and numbers are computing which is really not thinking I think at least at Koviashuvik it is not thinking.

I think at Koviashuvik it is not thinking. It is computing symbols of ideas but it is not thinking.

*   *   *

On the end of my nylon line singing through liquefied gasses I feel the great fish swing his head from side to side to release the hook that ties us through the arching rod pulling my wrist.

He turns silver and gold on the surface in flying crystal jewels above the roiling water I see the sun repeated and we shall eat the sun repeated and after supper I shall write the professor and ask how to program the idea of courage for the computer.

4
Being There
Where reality is real

After several winters in our summer cabin on the shore, we built a winter home two miles away in the spruce trees. Two hundred feet above the lake we built our cabin where it is twenty degrees warmer when it is fifty degrees below zero on the lake shore.

Thirty degrees below zero is warm. It is warm because warmth is something we feel after it has been fifty degrees below zero.

Fifty degrees below zero is on the Fahrenheit scale. On the Centigrade scale it is forty-five degrees below zero Celsius, but we are on the human scale.

Sometimes the human scale seems to be the same as the Centigrade or Fahrenheit scales but not very often. Not when the wind blows. When the wind blows there is a scale for chill factor. Even with a chill factor scale we are still on the human scale. At Koviashuvik we never forget we are on the human scale.

*   *   *

Anyway, we built our winter cabin of logs two hundred feet above the lake and called it the Palace. We called it the Palace because it was bigger than our shore cabin and it was warmer by twenty degrees. It was bigger by four feet in the same way that it was warmer if we used numbers. But at Koviashuvik we do not need a ruler to understand space nor a thermometer to know if we are cold.

When the grizzly bear arrived, early in the spring, we no longer called the winter cabin the Palace. We called it the Bear's Den.

I have already told how he tore up our cabin five times in one summer. Five times he raided our cabin so we called it the Bear's Den. Now I am calling it our winter home because that is what it is.

It is important to give things names. We do not know what a thing is unless we give it a name. That does not always make it what it is. I once stayed in a motel called Paradise, which should have been called Purgatory.

I wonder if the motel could have continued in business if it were called Purgatory. I don't think so, but it did have the wrong name. The City of the Angels in California has the wrong name and many other things in America have the wrong name.

*   *   *

When we were visiting America, which I will tell about later, people asked us what we did in the winter besides eat and sleep. I said we fed the fire.

When I said we fed the fire, someone would always ask is that all you do? And we would say we talk a lot and read a lot to each other.

Yes, we read. When Billie is working on a skin or rug I read to her and when I am using my hands she reads to me. We read to each other a lot, but mostly we talk about what we have read.

We have much to talk about because one winter we read *The Story of Civilization* which took Will and Ariel Durant most of their lives to write in eleven volumes. There was a lot to talk about.

In the meantime I ran a trapline over several miles and Billie baked and we are writers and we play cribbage.

*   *   *

Cribbage is a game to be played mostly in Alaska because there are so many cribbage boards in Alaska that are not boards. They are walrus tusks with holes drilled in them by Eskimos to sell to tourists to put on their mantels outside of Alaska.

Do people play cribbage with walrus tusks outside of Alaska? I don't know, but Billie and I play cribbage. Nearly every night we play cribbage with a cribbage board made in Hong Kong with holes drilled by Chinese.

It is interesting that we do not play cribbage with a walrus tusk in Alaska. We do not use a walrus tusk because we have a wooden Chinese cribbage board and do not have a mantel. We do not have a mantel because our log cabin is heated by a Yukon stove and a mantel is for a fireplace. We do not have a fireplace in our cabin because it would let more heat out in the wintertime than it would put in.

Anyway we play a lot of cribbage because a friend sent us a cribbage board with holes drilled by Chinese in Hong Kong. We learned that cribbage was invented by Sir John Suckling, an Englishman, who never visited Alaska.

We have a Scrabble board and play rummy and a game the Eskimos call Five Card. Mostly we play cribbage in

Alaska because we have a cribbage board made by Chinese in Hong Kong.

*   *   *

Yes, we trap.

In the winter I usually run a trapline. In Alaska we say we run a trapline when we mean showshoe a trapline which I did for six years before we had a snow machine.

Now I run a snowmobile but I still have to snowshoe a trail before I can run a snow machine on the trapline.

It is interesting that in America people run everything. They run their homes, their business, their lives and other people's lives. Everywhere people are running.

Well, trapping is one of the things we do in the winter. I set traps for wolves and lynx and wolverine, but mostly I use snares which is called trapping in Alaska because a snare is a trap. If you are caught in a snare you are trapped.

*   *   *

A wolverine is not easy to trap. When I was a marriage counselor I heard a lot about being trapped. People would talk about how they were trapped by their job or their children. They felt caught in a psychological snare which is how I trap wolverines. I use a psychological snare.

I make my sets at the base of a spruce tree. Under the snow I hide my traps and the wolverine springs these traps and urinates on them to show his contempt at the hidden traps. At least it seems like contempt.

Then I have another bait high in the tree, a psychological snare in the branches. Yes, a psychological snare because the wolverine does not expect the real snare after springing the hidden traps. He is caught in the snare which is not only psychological but real. A real snare in the branches.

In the academic world we used to debate the meaning of the real. We debated whether the world was finite or infinite. Because this was an academic question it was debated.

In winter at Koviashuvik infinity is finite. If the fire goes out infinity is real.

We feed the fire because reality is real at Koviashuvik.

*   *   *

Then there is Thanksgiving.

Thanksgiving comes after the sun goes. The sun disappears as the earth tips and hides the sun in the south for more than two months. We do not see the sun for seventy-seven days.

For seventy-seven days we have no direct sunlight. We see its light on the moon and the snow sparkles from reflected sunlight from the moon and stars. Stars are suns.

*   *   *

In winter we are aware of outer space from where the cold comes. Up there the aurora flows along magnetic lines like expanding colors of oil on water. I think about charmed quarks and black holes as I snowshoe across the frozen lake.

I listen to my snowshoes crunch the ice crystals and am delighted that sub-atomic particles have charm. I accepted their charm before Bjorken and Glashow gave the quantum number its name.

Somewhere up there between the glittering stars is a black hole which Kip Thorne of Cal Tech called a marvelously simply object because the matter that collapsed in the making of the black hole simply disappeared. Disappeared into a singularity.

Now that I know where matter goes, I have only to consider where it comes from. That brings me back to Thanksgiving.

*   *   *

Like everyone else in America we eat on Thanksgiving Day.

One year we had grizzly bear roast. Usually we eat moose for our basic dish because we have moose meat frozen in the cache. The year we had grizzly bear we had moose meat frozen in the cache but we preferred the roast grizzly because it was special. We also ate roast ptarmigan and canned yams flown in earlier and a sauce Billie made from lingonberries which are called low bush cranberries in Alaska. Botanists call them vaccinium *vitis-islea* but nobody else does. We had fresh sourdough bread and dressing and blueberry pie and wine we had saved for special occasions because Thanksgiving is a special occasion.

*   *   *

The year we had grizzly bear on Thanksgiving was more than a special occasion because we had unexpected guests. Any guest is unexpected at Koviashuvik after freeze-up. A small plane on skis zoomed over our cabin and after landing on the frozen lake our neighbor and his Eskimo wife ate grizzly bear with us.

Anyone who lives in the Brooks Range is a neighbor in an area the size of Italy. Everyone is a neighbor because there are not many of us. Like a small town, we know who our neighbors are and what they are doing. Our neighbor was a bounty hunter.

From the air he flew his Supercub while Mamie shot wolves from the back seat. Mamie flew shotgun and that was how they made their living before the bounty on wolves was removed. They were bounty hunters.

Billie and I were opposed to the bounty and aerial hunting of any kind. We said so and wrote letters and the bounty was removed and hunting from the air is now illegal and Earl is dead and Mamie is living in Fairbanks.

But we remember that Thanksgiving Day because we ate grizzly bear and had unexpected guests and we liked them and it was a special occasion.

*   *   *

Another special occasion is the shortest day of the year when the earth seems to stand still before it slowly tips back toward the sun. It was the day we put up our Christmas tree.

It was not a simple thing to put up our Christmas tree. We raised it in the middle of the frozen lake on the shortest day of the year one hundred miles north of the Arctic Circle in the middle of a frozen lake. We raised our tree, an eighteen foot spruce tree festooned with metal bangles of tin can lids. We raised it in the winter dark as the earth stood still for that brief moment before tipping us back toward the sun.

This is what Christmas is all about. It is in the dark hours that hope is born.

*   *   *

Now I will tell about it:

It is the end of the shortest day of the year. Our fire is sputtering and snapping in the Yukon stove. Overhead the gasoline lantern gives a gentle hiss. Along with its gentle hiss it illuminates the soft brown of logs and cardboard and weathered wood.

Stretched out on the caribou skins of the spruce pole bed, and reading a book, Nuliak looks up and smiles. Nuliak is Eskimo for wife. Although Billie is not Eskimo, our life here in this northern wilderness is much like that of the inland Eskimos who hunted caribou here for thousands of years.

We recently returned from the center of the frozen lake where we raised our spruce tree while the earth paused before reversing itself to begin its tip back toward the sun.

The sun disappeared over a month ago but its reflected light has been shining back from a waxing moon which is now full. Today the moon did not set. It passed behind Mount Truth's rocky spire at noon to reappear a few minutes later in a sky where sunrise and sunset meet to scramble wisps of mares' tails into as many colors as the tundra after a first frost.

*　　*　　*

It is now late afternoon but not dark because the moon is high and the shadow of our sled trail marks the surface of the lake like a crack in white marble. Like a crack in white marble, the sled trail leads from the lone tree we erected on the snow covered ice to our small cabin. We sense the earth swinging back.

We know the earth is back in its swing toward summer and we are tired and relaxed and content. I feel a contentment as I look through the cabin window to where our lantern light is reproduced as golden sparkles from reflecting crystals of snow. I am relaxed and content because this has been a day of great moment once recognized around the world. Once it was recognized by everyone, or nearly everyone, before we became too civilized to sense the importance of this day.

*　　*　　*

Yesterday, following the weather report from a Fairbanks radio station, the announcer reported a loss of one minute of sunlight and it had an ominous ring. To me it had an ominous ring. My reaction was primitive and irrational. I considered it irrational.

Now, I do not think it was irrational, maybe primitive but not irrational. I thought about tomorrow and about the day after and all the days to come. Then I looked at the calendar on the wall where WINTER SOLSTICE was printed in the square box which represented December the twenty-first. I was uneasy.

*   *   *

Why was I uneasy, I wondered. It was interesting that I was uneasy. Then I understood. It was the word "represented." "Represented" was the word, it was the key. That box was not December twenty-first. It was only a symbol, a representation of a period of time constructed by humans for convenience. A construction by people for convenience in coordinating their activities. Only a convenience.

*   *   *

When you live like inland Eskimos in the isolation of an arctic wilderness, knowledge takes on unique dimensions. When you were trained as a scientist, as I was, it does.

Since I was trained as a scientist, I knew that it was really a gamble that the earth would stop by the twenty-first and tip its northern hemisphere back toward the sun. Even though the odds were very high, I knew it was a gamble.

I knew it was a gamble because all that science can really say about such phenomena is that what usually happens will probably happen again under like conditions. That is all that science can say. It is a great faith.

Yes, it is a great faith by which we function, like my faith that I will live to be ninety. It is a faith because I can be trampled by a moose or slip on the ice or freeze to death tomorrow. Even if I don't like to think about it, it can happen.

*   *   *

Anyway, it was with these thoughts that I followed my trapline while the afternoon stars came out and the sub-zero frost on my whiskers pulled the skin around my mouth. I thought of bonfires once built on the mountains of northern Europe and the great yule logs cut and evergreen mistletoe and holly gathered as a stay against the dark.

As my snowshoes rhythmically crunched along the trail, I recalled a ceremony. I recalled a rain ceremony in New Mexico.

It was a ceremony in midsummer where my Pueblo Indian friend danced with his people rattling gourds. He rattled painted gourds and danced to the beat of a tom-tom. Yes, he danced to the beat of a tom-tom and held a doctor's degree in biology and I said, you don't think this will bring rain do you? He smiled and said, I don't dance for rain but it will rain. And it did.

I said, it would have rained whether there was a ceremony or not. It would have rained anyway. And he said, maybe so. He smiled and said, maybe so.

*   *   *

Last night I iced the sled runners for today.

We were up early. Billie and I were up early to use the short light of day. As soon as the sourdough pancakes were eaten I took the sled and my ax up the hill to cut a spruce.

The tree was carefully selected. It had to have a younger tree growing close by to replace it. We never cut a tree without a replacement, never. It had to be straight and tall.

We needed a special tree for such a momentous occasion. We found it growing on the hillside a hundred yards from the trail. Its frozen wood accepted my ax as if it were summer and I rolled the spruce onto the sled with ease. It rolled onto the sled with ease.

While I was bringing the tree, Billie was attaching kerosene and coffee can lids to rawhide thongs. She was tying thongs to metal scraps to decorate our tree with cans we'd used to store our food and bring light to our lamp. She made bangles to decorate our tree.

Then we tramped a trail and pulled the tree-burdened sled out on the flat expanse of the frozen lake surrounded by its frame of mountains.

Surrounded by mountains, I chipped a hole in the ice and we raised our tree while the earth stood still.

*   *   *

Did the earth stand still I wonder. Every year I wonder.

Anyway, as the world slowly began its swing back toward the sun-warmed days of summer, we returned to our snug cabin for caribou and coffee. We pulled the empty sled back across the frozen lake to our cabin where we took off our parkas and stirred up the fire.

Coals now glow like the sun in our Yukon stove and I wonder. Did we stop the earth and turn it toward summer? We are tipping back.

Yes, again we are tipping back. And we now have a Christmas tree and a glittering marker for the bush pilot who will fly in our Christmas mail.

More important, we have a symbol. It is only a representation. We know it is only a representation but it is a far better one than the square box marked on the calendar because we were there.

*   *   *

This is what our life is about at Koviashuvik.

Being there.

The concept of the environment stands before us as a problem to be solved. Can we convert it into a question to be experienced?

JACOB NEEDLEMAN

5
The Great Blue Range
And a little bit more

Break-up comes like an avalanche. Rivers roar. Birds fill valleys with song. Ducks and geese call. Loons laugh on the lakes. Terns and falcons hover over myriad ponds glistening with iridescent wings of newly hatched insects.

This is spring in the Brooks Range.

Summer is plunging waterfalls and hanging green valleys. A white Dall sheep stands motionless on a pinnacle of rock high above turbulent water. Summer is great billowing clouds above mountains with rainstorms, sleet, hail, lightning and fires. Smoke drifts up the valleys. Clouds of mosquitos hum above the muskeg and fireweed is crimson in the foothills.

In mid-summer the sun never sets below the horizon.

With the first frosts of autumn, mountains sing with orange alder, yellow willow and golden birches. Antlers flash white as a moose lifts its dripping head from the marsh. A grizzly bear, golden brown in the sun, fattens on blueberries where flocks of ptarmigan share the bounty of cloudberries and scarlet lingonberries.

Then the cold seals the rivers and creeks. Stars glitter above crags no one has climbed. There echoes down canyons the howl of wolves at their kill. The aurora twists, turns and dances across the sky above a now silent range. The long winter begins.

This is the Brooks Range. This was the last major wilderness on the North American continent when we made it our home. It still is.

*   *   *

This great blue range, in which we live, sweeps east of the sun and west of the moon across northern Alaska. The mountains stretch across the state of Alaska between Canada and the Bering Sea. The Brooks Range is the dramatic northern end of a ridge in the earth's crust, a wrinkle in the earth, that projects above the ice of Antarctica at the southern end of the world.

This cordillera begins eleven thousand miles from us by dipping beneath the sea which divides the Atlantic and Pacific oceans. In Tierra Del Fuego, the mountains rise to snow covered peaks which extend north as the Andes of South America. The Andes of South America become the Sierra Madre of Central America and Mexico. We call it the Rocky Mountains in the United States. In Canada we also call it the Rocky Mountains, but not in Alaska.

In Alaska this great wrinkle in the earth's crust turns west to form the Brooks Range north of the Arctic Circle.

North of the Arctic Circle, the upthrust which began at the other end of the earth stretches five hundred miles in an escarpment, fifty to one hundred and fifty miles wide, from Canada to the Bering Sea. The great blue range sweeps five hundred miles across the state of Alaska north of the Arctic Circle.

In these mountains of mystery is our home.

*   *   *

Between the Yukon River and the Arctic Ocean, these mountains are still largely unexplored. They have had visitors because aircraft have made the Brooks Range accessible to geologists, hunters and fishermen. There is now an oil pipeline crossing the range but it is still a wilderness.

This great range, about the size of Italy, is still uninhabited except for a few inland Eskimos and Indians and a handful of white Americans who manage to survive by trapping and panning gold from its icy streams. We trap and pan gold but mostly we are writers. Today we are mostly writers.

*   *   *

The first white man to glimpse the Brooks Range is believed to have been Sir John Franklin, the famous English explorer. Franklin was sailing west along the Arctic coast from the mouth of the Mackenzie river in 1826. He was sponsored by the Hudson's Bay Company. While sailing west along the coast, he wrote in his journal that he could see rocky mountains in the distance. This was the first reported sighting on record.

Franklin was sailing west to reach Point Barrow where he planned to meet with Captain F. M. Beechy, Captain of Her Majesty's Ship *Blossom*. Captain Beechy was exploring the Alaskan coast from the west.

Franklin was stopped by ice just east of Beechy Point at Return Reef. One hundred and forty-six miles from the Eskimo village at Point Barrow he was stopped by the ice.

Franklin later disappeared in the Arctic. Today Franklin

is given credit for finding the Brooks Range. This is interesting because the Brooks Range was never lost. However, Franklin was lost. Sir John Franklin and his whole expedition were lost and never found.

*   *   *

More than forty years after Sir John Franklin first saw the Brooks Range, Robert Kennicott saw the range as a barrier to the Western Union Telegraph Company's plan to construct an overland telegraph line from the United States to Asiatic and European capitals.

Robert Kennicott was a young scientist and explorer from Chicago. In 1865 it was not believed possible to lay a cable under the Atlantic Ocean. Kennicott was employed to superintend a scouting and exploration of the northern region along the Yukon for the telegraph to Europe by way of Asia.

At the age of thirty, Kennicott had founded the Chicago Academy of Sciences and Natural History and had made an extensive journey to the mouth of the Mackenzie River on the Arctic Ocean in 1862. He was collecting for the Academy. From the Mackenzie, he had crossed down the Porcupine River to Fort Yukon on the Yukon River in Alaska. He remained south of the Brooks Range for a season studying the area and the people in the vicinity.

While he was there, he became convinced that the Yukon River was the upper part of the same river that flowed into the Bering Sea, a river which the Eskimos and Russians called the Kwikpak. Kwikpak means big river in Eskimo. It is.

Both the Russians and the Eskimos called the river the Kwikpak. However, at Fort Yukon, the Hudson's Bay Company trappers called it the Yukon. Even though it is one of the world's largest rivers, it is no longer called the Kwikpak. Everyone calls it the Yukon.

*   *   *

Two years later, in 1865, Kennicott and his party of explorers landed at the Russian American trading post of St. Michael on the Bering Sea coast. During that winter, they crossed the Unaliklik Portage to the village of Nulato on the Kwikpak River near the junction of the Koyokuk River. There they began preparation for the explorations up river toward Fort Yukon after spring break-up.

For Kennicott, the range to the north was an insurmountable obstacle. He wrote: "Nothing was seen but continuous ranges of snow-covered mountains rolling one over another for God knows how many miles."

*   *   *

It was early May of 1886, while waiting for the ice to go out of the river, that Kennicott failed to return one morning from a sand bank where he was making compass bearings of landmarks.

Members of his party found him dead. He was sprawled on the figures he had made in the sand and they reported that he had died of heart failure. In his early thirties, he died of heart failure before he finished the trip to Fort Yukon.

How many people die before they finish their trip?

*   *   *

Kennicott is now part of history. Later, the Kennecott Copper Company was named after him, misspelling his name. However, he is remembered in Chicago as the founder of the Chicago Academy of Sciences and Natural History, and we remember him as part of the history of the Brooks Range. But mostly people do not remember people who are dead, at least not very often.

*   *   *

A few months after Kennicott's death, a twenty-one-year-old member of the Scientific Corps of the Western

Telegraph Company, by the name of William Healey Dall, landed at St. Michael to take up Kennicott's cable route exploration.

Young William Dall believed Kennicott was murdered. He believed Kennicott was poisoned by Russian criminals because Alaska was a penal colony and Dall was convinced that those sent across the Bering Sea were too bad to be exiled to Siberia. Siberia was not punishment enough, so they were sent to Alaska where Dall believed they were responsible for Kennicott's sudden death.

Anyway, that winter Dall accompanied by Frederick Whymper, the artist and author, along with Major Frank Ketchum and Mike La Barge, crossed the Unaliklik Portage to Nulato to prepare his party for the ascent of the Yukon River in the spring of 1867.

In mid-winter, Ketchum and La Barge started ahead with dog teams and continued to the headwaters of the Yukon. Later, the following summer, they returned to Fort Yukon and reported the existence of several large lakes, one of which now bears the name of La Barge.

People like to have lakes and mountains named for them. Yearning for immortality takes many forms.

*　　*　　*

William Dall and Frederick Whymper followed Ketchum and La Barge in small boats after break-up. They reached the Hudson's Bay Post at Fort Yukon in the latter part of June. On his trip, Dall could see the mountains of the Brooks Range to the north. He could see the mountains which were not then named, but he assumed it was the same range Sir John Franklin had seen from the Arctic Ocean. It was.

*　　*　　*

Dall and his party returned to St. Michael and upon their arrival learned that an Atlantic cable had been successful. They learned that a cable had been laid under the Atlantic Ocean and their overland project had been abandoned. Although the project had been abandoned, Dall remained in the vicinity of Nulato through the summer of 1868. He spent the time gathering data and collecting for the Smithsonian Institution before leaving that autumn for San Francisco. Eventually, the white Dall sheep of Alaska and the Brooks Range were named after him.

To most people a Dall sheep is a Dall sheep like a white horse is a white horse. So much for names and immortality.

*　　*　　*

Alaska was purchased from Russia in 1867. However, it was nearly twenty years later, in 1885, that the first explorations into the Brooks Range were made after Alaska became a United States Territory.

It was considered a mistake to purchase Alaska. It was called Seward's Folly because Seward promoted the purchase and he was ridiculed for it. Today he is not ridiculed. Today we think he was wise. He was.

*　　*　　*

In 1885 Lieutenant Henry Tureman Allen was fresh out of West Point. He had just graduated from the Military Academy, and with an exploration team made up of a sergeant, a private, and two civilians, set out to discover for the War Department what we had bought from Russia. Yes, the War Department wanted to know what we had bought and Lieutenant Allen was asked to gather "all information which will be valuable and important, especially to the military branch of the government."

Lieutenant Allen named the central mountains of the range for William Endicott, who was Secretary of War in President Cleveland's administration. It was a generation later, however, before it was known that half a dozen separate chains of mountains, now called the Endicotts,

the Philip Smith, and Romanzof mountains, were part
of a single connected range. The range was finally named
in 1925 for Dr. Alfred Hulse Brooks, the Chief Geologist
of the United States Geological Survey.

These, and many other names, are printed in bold letters on today's maps of the range but, as Alfred Habdank Skarbek Korzybski pointed out, the map is not the
territory.

*   *   *

When Lieutenant Allen traveled up the Yukon River
in 1885, it was not in his plans to explore or charter in
the Brooks Range. As I said, an explorer does not know
what he is exploring until he explores it. However, when
Allen encountered the Koyokuk River, where it flowed
into the Yukon, and traveled up it over one thousand
miles from the sea, he found the Koyokuk to be three
hundred yards wide and fourteen feet deep. He assumed
it must flow from some immense lake in the northern
flats. This he assumed. So, for a week he and his party
poled upstream to a large tributary, later called the John
River.

In his journal, Allen speaks of his first becoming aware
of cold winds that could come only from snowy peaks.
He traveled up the John River to where he found himself
in the central Brooks Range with white-topped mountains stretching east and west along the northern horizon.

Today, a tributary of the John, called the Allen River,
records his name in the range.

*   *   *

Lieutenant Allen did not know it but in the same year
a Navy expedition reached the Brooks Range under
Lieutenant George M. Stoney, who headed a party of
six officers and twelve men.

With his men, Lieutenant Stoney traveled up the
Kobuk River in the western Brooks Range and estab-

lished a winter camp. They built a cabin for the winter and called it Fort Cosmos. There his men spent the long months of darkness while Lieutenant Stoney and Ensign Howard, with four Eskimos, continued on to the upper Noatak River. They reached the upper Noatak in December of 1885 and established contact with the inland Eskimos.

After meeting with these inland Eskimos, Stoney wanted to continue through the range to the north and descend the Coleville River to the Arctic coast. The Eskimos refused to guide him. They refused to guide him because they knew the northern Brooks Range was too desolate at that time of year for travel. The Eskimos knew, even if Stoney didn't know, they knew.

*   *   *

Stoney's explorations took him to the head of the Kobuk River and over ridges to the Alatna River. He hiked across the top of the range to Chandler Lake, in the area north of timber line, where even dwarf willow becomes scarce for firewood.

There Stoney purchased a sled from a Nunamiut Eskimo, camped at Chandler Lake, and burned it for cooking fuel. The effect on the sled maker was such that the story of the crazy man is still told today among the Nunamiut. Although Stoney maintained that the sled belonged to him and he could do what he chose with it, his act was incomprehensible to the Eskimo. It was not only incomprehensible, to them it was immoral. If Stoney had eaten the sled it would have been better understood. Even to me, it would be better understood.

*   *   *

In spring it was the custom for many inland Nunamiut families to travel down to the Arctic coast to trade. Ensign Howard went with them. Traveling with the Eskimos in 1886, Ensign Howard finally accomplished, with relative ease, Lieutenant Stoney's desire that his expedition reach the Arctic Ocean.

Today, Howard Pass records his name as the first white explorer to cross the Brooks Range.

*   *   *

From Lieutenant Stoney's reports, his party was caught by the incredible grandeur of the mountains, the deep gorges, waterfalls, wide valleys and turbulent rivers.

Stoney notes that his men consumed two thousand five hundred pounds of caribou meat, supplemented by ptarmigan, geese, ducks and snowshoe hares. The rivers and lakes were filled with grayling, trout, salmon and sheefish. The land was hard and forbidding, yet gentle and giving of its bounty.

This is the contrast which gives the range its character. Even today, it is this contrast which gives character to the great blue range. Everything is contrast.

*   *   *

All who speak of the Brooks Range stress its combination of strength and vulnerability, from the garden appearance of its valleys to its jagged, gaunt peaks, from broad, winding rivers to roaring torrents and leaping waterfalls, from warm days when the sun never sets and the smell of blossoms and songs of birds fill the air, to the frozen silence of the long winter night with temperatures between forty and seventy degrees below zero.

The Brooks Range is not only the greatest wilderness on the American continent, it is the most fragile. Where spruce trees take two hundred years to grow head high, recovery from a fire is the process of ages.

Very little decays or sinks into the earth. Very little disappears. Even trails and campsites from early prospectors and gold miners remain visible scars today. Cans and bottles are still where they were tossed over eighty years ago.

*   *   *

In 1893 a prospector by the name of Johnnie Folger discovered gold on the Middle Fork of the Koyokuk River at Tramway Bar. Where a tributary entered the river he found the yellow metal in paying quantities, but little notice was taken until the great stampede of 1898 brought 80,000 people north from all over the world.

From all over the world, people came because the Klondike and Dawson gold strikes of 1897 had been reported. At Dawson and at Klondike most of the good claims had already been staked, so in the late summer of 1898 some two hundred overflow prospectors made their way north of the Arctic Circle into the foothills of the Brooks Range. There they staked out claims on the South and Middle Forks of the Koyokuk River and were caught by an early freeze-up. They were marooned for the long winter night.

Most of the prospectors survived the winter. But as soon as the river broke up in the spring, they pulled up stakes and drifted down the Koyokuk to the Yukon leaving their campsites and cabins for the hardier and more permanent miners who followed.

Other prospectors made their way into the remote canyons of the range but, with the exception of a few trading settlements serving miners and trappers, the range remained the wilderness it was when Sir John Franklin first sighted its peaks in 1826.

*   *   *

Most of the trading settlements were transient. Today only names remain. Only the traders' names.

Gordon C. Bettles opened a store at the mouth of the John River on the Koyokuk in the fall of 1899. The settlement which grew up around it was named after him.

In 1901, William Plummer and the Northern Commercial Company opened stores at the mouth of Slate Creek on the Middle Fork of the Koyokuk River. It was called Coldfoot.

Coldfoot reached its peak in 1902 when it rated two roadhouses, two stores and seven saloons. It also boasted a gambling hall and ten prostitutes.

With the discovery of a rich strike on Nolan Creek, north of Coldfoot, a community grew up at the site of Wright's old roadhouse at the mouth of Wiseman Creek. This settlement was first called Wright's, then it was called Nolan and finally Wiseman.

Wiseman soon replaced Coldfoot as the trading center.

By 1915 Wiseman was serving as many as three hundred whites and a hundred natives in a fifteen thousand square mile area.

*   *   *

The population declined after 1916 when the richest claims had been mined out and World War One raised the price of wages outside Alaska. Today only a handful of people live in Wiseman.

Coldfoot disappeared as a community but retained its name as a trans-Alaska pipeline construction camp. Original Bettles also has gone. Today the name remains attached to the government airfield maintained six miles up the Koyokuk River from the old townsite.

The name, Bettles, is now attached to the community at the airfield. It is our post office. Although it is eighty miles away by air from Koviashuvik, it is still our post office.

*   *   *

It was from the writings of Robert Marshall that I became interested in the Brooks Range. It was Bob Marshall who made the range known to many. He drew maps, named mountains, photographed and wrote about a landscape he felt surpassed the grandeur of Yellowstone or Yosemite.

When he was Director of Forestry of the Office of Indian Affairs, and later as Chief of the Division of Recreation and Lands of the United States Forest Service, until his sudden death in 1939, Bob Marshall's voice was heard by all who were concerned with wilderness. His voice is still heard today through the Wilderness Society. It was largely through his efforts that the Wilderness Society came into being.

Marshall's explorations in Alaska were under his own sponsorship. Billie and I keep our own sponsorship. Like Bob Marshall, we keep our own sponsorship so we are not restricted.

*   *   *

It was Bob Marshall's zest and love for exploration which brought him on six different expeditions into the arctic wilderness of the central Brooks Range.

Because he was reared with a sense of public obligation, Marshall felt that exploration should have a social justification. Therefore, the rationale for his original trips into these mountains, was, as he put it, to add to the scientific knowledge of tree growth at northern timber line and to study civilization in the Arctic.

His study of civilization in the Arctic produced the book *Arctic Village,* a study of the community of miners and Eskimos living in and about the community of Wiseman. It won the Literary Guild Award in the nineteen thirties and was a best seller.

In his study of tree growth, he planted white spruce seeds north of timber line while exploring the headwaters of the Koyokuk River in order to test his theory of northern migration of trees in the central Brooks Range.

*   *   *

For Robert Marshall his experiments were secondary to his joy in exploring an incredible wilderness which he found more spectacular than the Rocky Mountains or the Sierra Nevada.

After his second trip into the range, in the early nineteen thirties, he wrote, "An excuse for exploration no longer seemed necessary for me. I frankly acknowledged that the justification for exploration in modern times must be found primarily in what it contributes to the personal happiness of the explorer rather than what it may add to the well-being of the human race."

*   *   *

There is no doubt that the great blue range enhanced Bob Marshall's happiness. His journals are expressions of delight in the discovery of a world in all its timeless elemental strength and beauty.

He named one hundred and thirty-seven places in the central region of the range. He named mountains, rivers and creeks, such as *Bombardment Creek, Rumbling Mountain* and *Mount Doonerak*. He gave the designation, *Gates of the Arctic,* to a pass on the North Fork of the Koyokuk River where it flows between jagged pinnacles which he called *Frigid Crags,* and a great tower of rock he named *Boreal Mountain.*

*   *   *

Today the great blue range is no longer a lonely forgotten land. *Gates of the Arctic* is the name of a National Park in the area.

With the opening of the Sagwon Oil Field on the Arctic coast and the development of copper mines in the foothills of the western mountains, the Brooks Range has experienced a surge of commercial interest which threatens this last great wilderness. A trans-Alaska pipeline haul road has been opened to the public and other routes for roads have been surveyed. There is still serious discussion of a railroad to be constructed to the copper mines near Shungnak, at Bornite, on the Kobuk River.

This fragile arctic mountain fastness may soon become another development in our insatiable need to exploit the land. Even Gates of the Arctic National Park is itself a threat.

*   *   *

If we view the Brooks Range from a national or world perspective, it is obvious that its greatest value is its wilderness character.

The pioneer conditions still found north of the Arctic Circle have been largely destroyed in the continental United States. Even in Alaska, development is still oriented towards roads and industries. Yet there is hope.

There is hope in the growing millions who feel that the value of wilderness, with its primitive conditions and difficult means of transportation, is basic to those human qualities which have given our nation and its people their particular character.

Even so, there are other millions who would domesticate everything if they could. They speak of a concern for the wilderness, but would domesticate it like they domesticate everything else.

*   *   *

Alaska is still unique in that only here can the emotional values of the frontier be preserved. Only here can there still be found a really sizeable area free from roads and industries where frontier conditions still remain. Only by good fortune has the Brooks Range been too remote from markets for successful industry. Only by the good fortune of its remoteness has the population been too small and scattered to justify the cost of roads.

Travel is still primarily by air as it has been for centuries for other fellow creatures who can fly.

*   *   *

Millions of excited birds arrive each spring. They arrive soon after break-up. From here an inner call is heard by multitudes of migrating water fowl. Some, like the Arctic tern, fly eleven thousand miles from Antarctica for their courtship and mating. Here their young will be born as their parents were before them. Loons, swans, cranes, plovers, geese and ducks by the thousands arrive at the place of their year's fulfillment.

No one knows why the Arctic has such a call for animals that move with the seasons. Perhaps in a warmer age the animal center of population was here and their descendants have the urge to return. Perhaps it is because the north has been remote, a place apart. Or, perhaps it is a response to the country itself, a place where there is a fresh crispness in the air and the sun shines night and day but circles the horizon instead of climbing over the zenith so that light and shadow always have the fresh touch of morning.

*   *   *

By the time frost flowers form on icy marshes and ponds, most of the birds will have gone.

Cobalt blue mountains tower into a turquoise sky where stars appear in mid-afternoon and the only sound is the click of a thousand hooves as a herd of caribou crosses the ice.

In mid-winter it is a prehistoric land, silent and motionless except for the aurora streaming across the sky. The only boundary seems to be the stars. Here infinity is not a philosophical concept. It is a daily experience.

My God
it just occurred to me
underneath
our clothes
everyone on this bus
is stark naked

RIC MASTEN

6
Visit to America
East of the sun and west of the moon

The interviewer asked where we were from.

I said, "We live at Koviashuvik in the wilderness of northern Alaska."

"Where is that?" he said. "I mean, specifically, where is Koviashuvik?"

When he said "specifically," I did not know how to answer. I knew he wanted me to say something about geography but that would not be the right answer. So I said, "We think of it as east of the sun and west of the moon."

"Well," he said, "that is not a very satisfactory description."

I said, "It is not just a place. It is also a time."

He said, "O.K. then, when is it?"

I said, "Koviashuvik is Eskimo, time and place of joyfulness in the present moment."

There was a long pause while the interviewer looked

at his notebook. He looked at his notebook like he was trying to find something. It was not on the page. He looked up, swallowed, and said, "I gather that it is in Alaska."

"It can be other places as well." I said.

"How can it be two places at the same time?" he asked.

"That is a question," I said. "That is a most important question."

That is the question we took with us when we visited America.

*   *   *

It is a strange experience to visit the United States when you have been living in the United States, but not really in the United States, because people in America do not think of Alaska as really in the United States although they do think of it but not very often.

Because we have been living in the wilderness north of the Arctic Circle in Alaska, even people in Anchorage, which considers itself the only city of stature in Alaska, think of us as visitors. Anchorage is in the United States but not really like people think of Alaska outside of Alaska. People outside of Alaska think of Alaska as a wilderness. It is a wilderness, except that the real wilderness is the United States.

The United States is the wilderness if you live in the Brooks Range and visit the United States as we did one winter.

*   *   *

Before we went outside, which is everything outside of Alaska, we gave our lecture and showed our slides and film to our neighbors at the village of Bettles.

Bettles is our post office and is eighty miles from Koviashuvik if you are in a bush plane. If you are on snowshoes, or hiking over the mountains, it is more than one hundred and fifty miles.

In New York and Boston no one knew how many miles it was to anywhere nearby. They only knew how many minutes it was. When we asked how far it was from LaGuardia Airport to Grand Central Station or from Wellesley to Boston, we were told how many minutes it was. In San Francisco it was twenty minutes to Berkeley and half an hour to the airport. We learned that distance is time in the United States.

*   *   *

When we arrived in Seattle, our friend Peter met us. He was minister of the University Unitarian Church and his hair was long. He had longer hair than when we had seen him last. Everyone was older, of course, but it was hair that I kept seeing. Some were grayer, but most were darker. Most were darker like Ronald Reagan, who is much older than I am. My hair was longer but there is no barber shop where I live in Alaska. It was interesting that everybody's hair was longer. No one had a crew cut like the one I had when we moved into the wilderness.

It was strange not to see snow. There was green grass beside the freeway and in front of houses near the University. It was green in Seattle. It rained.

*   *   *

The people who arranged for our lecture in Seattle were helpful. They took us to a small hotel near the University. It was in a residential area. We liked it but the office door was locked and the door had to be unlocked to let us in to register. We were told the door was kept locked all the time. If we wanted anything we were asked to ring the bell and the door would be unlocked for us.

Everything seemed locked in the United States, at least most buildings. The church where we lectured had padlocks with chains around the handles of the doors to the sanctuary. When the chains were removed to let us in, we were told that the church had been robbed two days before even though a new burglar alarm had been installed.

We lectured in the auditorium, which was where chains were around the door handles. We thought it strange to call it a sanctuary.

In Berkeley, California we stayed in the same motel room we occupied when we were outside four years before. The room had additional locks and the office was locked day and night so that we had to ring a bell in order to be recognized to pay our bill. We were told that no one walks alone at night in any of the large cities we visited.

People kept telling us of their concern at our living in the wilderness where we never lock a door or own a lock.

*　　*　　*

At the airport in Seattle our bags were searched with an X-ray and a disembodied voice told us where to go through doors into a car with no driver. Another voice told us to look at the chart to see when to get out for the right airline. Everyone obeyed the voice and no one talked to anyone else. It was strange after living freely in the wilderness.

*　　*　　*

We rented a car in San Francisco. Actually, we rented a car at the airport because it was so far to San Francisco from the airport that it was a good idea to rent a car if you are going to lecture in Berkeley and Walnut Creek and Marin County.

Time is not only distance in the United States, it is also money. In the wilderness of the United States you need to watch your money. We did not have to watch our money because we had a credit card to watch our money. However, we had to watch Visa watching our money because we were charged interest for watching our money. Still, it was better to have Visa watch our money than to worry about watching our money.

Then we drove across the Golden Gate to lecture in Marin County.

*   *   *

It was sunny when we drove across the Golden Gate Bridge. It took a long time because traffic moved slower than walking over tussocks on the tundra of northern Alaska. On the radio we heard the helicopter say that a jumper had left his car blocking bridge traffic but that it would soon be removed. Then the radio informed us that another jumper, who had not blocked traffic, missed the water at the north end of the bridge and was being taken to a hospital. We later learned that he was only bruised, which is remarkable because few people survive who jump from the Golden Gate Bridge. We were told that suicide attempts are always made from the bay side of the bridge, never facing the open sea. Of course.

Anyway, it was sunny and the hills across the bridge were green and seagulls drifted over the blue water. We talked in Marin about Koviashuvik, telling how it is Eskimo for time and place of joy.

*   *   *

We spoke in Walnut Creek and a mockingbird sang outside while we were talking and everyone was serious. They asked us how we had the courage to live in the wilderness north of the Arctic Circle where there was no doctor. Everywhere we went we were asked what we would do if we were sick or hurt since we had no phone or way to call for help. Everyone seemed to worry about this. Actually we found people were more worried for themselves, which was strange because they had phones and could always get help. Perhaps they worried for themselves because they were afraid of dying. No healthy person wants to die, at least most of us want to keep on living. But all of us are going to die sometime. Even at Koviashuvik we are going to die.

We are not afraid of dying but we do not like pain. If there is too much pain Billie and I will do the act of mercy for the other. If it is needed we will act, so we are not concerned with death like everyone in the United States seems concerned. In the United States we found people concerned with death but afraid to talk about it.

*   *   *

In Berkeley we visited the graduate theological seminary where I had been a professor during the free speech movement on the university campus. We drove down Telegraph Avenue where a friend of mine was clubbed to the sidewalk by state troopers as he watched people marching in protest to the war in Vietnam.

It is not like it was in the sixties. We saw few smiles on people's faces and there was little music in the air. There was a serious mood and the street is only one way now. In the sixties you could go both ways and there was music in the air and there were smiles. Even with the troopers you could go both ways in the sixties.

*   *   *

We had espresso coffee with my two sons at the north gate of the university campus and it was good being with them. We sat outside in the sun. We liked the sun but the traffic was so loud we could not talk or hear the sparrows that still nested in the eaves above the restaurant.

At Koviashuvik it was quiet until helicopters began flying through the wilderness to service the trans-Alaska pipeline. The oil pipeline was built for cars in the United States to get gasoline so that people could drive into the wilderness which once was quiet.

* * *

We liked San Francisco because San Francisco is San Francisco and never pretends to be anything else.

But San Francisco was different from the San Francisco we knew. It was different even though the sun was bright when we ate crab cocktails at Fisherman's Wharf. People were still flying kites at the Marina and the wind in the bay made the sails lean against the green shore of Angel Island over which I flew in the sixties to illegally scatter ashes of a friend who had worked there for the park service.

San Francisco was different because people had been shot at random. A boy had been charged with murder because he killed two other people he did not know. We knew his parents. The boy was deranged because his fiance was raped. He was sick and San Francisco was sick.

When we were there, San Francisco was sick and people were afraid to go out at night. Doors were double locked. When we lectured, the auditorium was not full. People called to say they would not go out at night because they were afraid. At the lecture, we were asked if we were afraid in the wilderness where the wolves howl at night and it is cold and the sun never shines for seventy-seven days. When we said no, they did not believe us.

* * *

Then we flew to Burbank, California, which is not Los Angeles, but is where the plane landed us for Los Angeles. Flying from San Francisco to Burbank, we could see snow on the Sierra Nevada Range across the San Joaquin Valley. We were delighted to see the snow and the mountains where we had camped and climbed. The high mountains were like Koviashuvik. If you hiked away from the roads it was like wilderness.

You can't hike in Los Angeles because Los Angeles is built for cars. When I was in Los Angeles over thirty years ago, it was becoming the model for other cities being built for cars. It is still the model for Phoenix, Albuquerque, and Anchorage, Alaska where people have moved to get away from Los Angeles.

*   *   *

We liked everybody we met on the west coast even though we did not really meet anyone. We did not really meet anyone because everyone we met was coping. We could not talk with them the way we talk with people in the bush, which is what they call the wilderness where we live at Koviashuvik. At Koviashuvik, we do not cope but everyone we met on the west coast was coping. It is hard to meet with anyone when everybody is coping.

When people were not coping they were dieting, which they also called coping. All across the United States people were dieting. Everywhere we went we were offered food. We were offered food where people were dieting and we ate it and it was good. While we ate, people were dieting.

Once we were asked if we were vegetarians. I said yes, but we could not digest the tundra and willows where we live without processing them. And so we ate tundra and willows processed, in the form of caribou and moose.

Only a few people smiled because they were concerned about cholesterol and wanted to know how we coped with saturated fats.

*   *   *

In Los Angeles I phoned to rent a car to drive to Redlands. The phone was not answered in Los Angeles because the rental exchange was in another part of the country. They said they would rent us a car in Los Angeles because we had a credit card. However, it was not the credit card they wanted, only the number on the card. We learned that our money was now a number like we are a number to the bank and to the Internal Revenue Service. This was interesting because it did not matter who rented the car. It was only the number. At Kovia-shuvik you are you and a number is a number.

*   *   *

We liked Redlands and we liked the people in the retirement community of Plymouth Village. We talked and showed our film to people who had lived long enough to know that Koviashuvik is not a place but a way of perceiving. Not everyone had lived long enough. A few of the oldest still thought age was wisdom and youth a time of life.

My mother lived in Plymouth Village and she was glad we were there to talk and show our slides. She had been north of the Arctic Circle to visit Koviashuvik but she was not sure that people believed that she had been there when she was eighty-six. When you are retired and old, people do not believe you did what you did like they do when you are young.

*   *   *

Then we flew to Phoenix and we liked it there because we had once lived there and friends were there and we stayed with them. They were young at heart even though their boy had recently drowned. They knew that he was dead although they did not want to believe that he was dead but they did believe that he was dead and they were young. Being young is not a time of life but a way to see.

As Ric Masten said:

> *so you want to live*
> *forever*
> *do you*

well then let us
now
freeze the sunset
and bore ourselves
to death.

*   *   *

We drove out to the village of Guadalupe at the east end of the South Mountains. The adobe houses were still there with chickens, dogs, dirt, outdoor privies and the mission with blue pigeons cooing in its belfry. There were more old car carcasses in the yards than there were before, and the main street was now paved. But the broad hipped Yaquis, in their blue jeans, were the same and they smiled.

Senator Barry Goldwater was in Phoenix because a helicopter clattered down to his hilltop home near Camelback Mountain and we knew it was where he lived because of the transmitting antenna which we had seen on television. Besides, everyone told us where Barry Goldwater lived. No one told us about Guadalupe.

*   *   *

At Arizona State University in Tempe, we talked with professors and students in the Department of Anthropology. We could not tell the students from the professors because they looked the same and talked the same. They asked about Eskimos who had died more than a thousand years before we moved into the Arctic. We tried to talk about our neighbors, who are Eskimo, but they wanted to talk about dead Eskimos so we did.

One professor, who was not a student, could not talk with us because he did not want to talk about Eskimos. He only wanted to talk about Eskimo teeth that had once belonged to Eskimos. We did not know about teeth that had belonged to Eskimos a thousand years ago. It was very interesting that he could not talk to us because we did not know about thousand-year-old teeth.

*   *   *

We lectured in Phoenix and many people came to hear us because we were on television and there was an article in the newspaper with our pictures. People were interested in Alaska but not to go there. They had moved to Phoenix to get away from the cold. At least we were entertainment.

Then we flew over the desert to Tucson on our way to Albuquerque.

*   *   *

Flying over the South Mountains south of Phoenix, we could see beyond the Gila River to Estrella Peak which I had climbed with Ed Heald before he was killed in World War II. Ed was killed off the coast of Alaska. He was flying a B24 bomber from the Aleutian Islands and never returned.

Ray and Joe never returned either, but they were not killed in Alaska. They were killed in Korea. Mark Kelley never returned. Neither did Jim nor Frank nor Walter from Vietnam. Neither did David, who put a hose into his car from the exhaust pipe, nor Harold, who died from an overdose because he did not want to be a soldier, nor Frank, who was called a schizophrenic and jumped off the Golden Gate Bridge.

Anyway, Estrella Peak reminded me of a lot of truth seekers who never returned. It also reminded us of the mountain peak we see from our cabin window at Koviashuvik in Alaska. It is called Mount Truth. Two thousand years ago Pontius Pilate asked what is truth?

*   *   *

Between Phoenix and Tucson we could not see the miles of giant saguaro cactus because we were too high, but we could see the freeway and the fields which used to be desert and the tailings from the mines. Then, from Tucson we flew over the mountains to Albuquerque, New Mexico.

*   *   *

Before landing at Albuquerque, we flew over the ammunition bunkers I helped to construct when I was with the Office of Scientific Research and Development.

Oppie was alive then and he was famous. He was called Doctor J. Robert Oppenheimer by those who did not know him and we were all young then. We were winning the war. We did. But after Hiroshima and Nagasaki we didn't.

Albuquerque was different but it was still Albuquerque. The university, where I had taught biology and which had given me a degree so I could teach biology, was no longer near the edge of town. There were no more horse-drawn wagons of firewood from Tijeras canyon being driven into town. Instead, there were freeways and high-rises and a cable car to the top of the Sandia Mountains.

We liked being in Albuquerque. Still, it was not like it was when the Indians wore velvet shirts with turquoise beads and silver conchos. You can still hear as much Spanish as English while people talk in the sun waiting for a bus. But today Albuquerque is more like Los Angeles.

*   *   *

We lectured in Albuquerque. Mostly we liked being with Lois Fay and her fifth and sixth graders in their open classroom. They were talking about Adventure Island, which they had invented. There, they were going to start a new civilization. They told us about how each person could only take a hundred pounds to Adventure Island. They told us what they would take, why some things were more important than others, and how they would govern themselves. They asked us what we would take and we told them about Koviashuvik, which is like Adventure Island, except that Koviashuvik is real.

We said that Koviashuvik told us what to take. It told us to take a knife, a rifle and an ax. It told us how to govern ourselves, because if we did not help each other and respect the animals we ate and the trees we cut we would die. Since they had not thought about what Adventure Island could tell them, we talked about it.

We talked about ecology but we did not call it ecology because ecology is really a way of thinking and not just what goes on between things and their environment.

A small boy with big eyes asked how Koviashuvik told us to take the things we did.

I said, "The same way as when I cut a tree the notch tells me where to swing the ax for the next cut."

He said, "Then it's like when I'm hungry, my stomach tells me to eat."

And I said, "Doesn't the clock tell you too?"

And he said, "Yes, and so does the lunch bell."

Then we all laughed. And that was epistemology but he did not know the word for it.

*   *   *

After we took off from Albuquerque, over the Monzano Mountains, the United States was cut up into squares and oblongs all the way to New York. Every time we looked out of the window it was brown, yellow and green in straight lines below the clouds.

In Alaska, when you fly north from Fairbanks there are no straight lines except the airstrips at Alakaket and Bettles.

We circled over New York City and it was clear. We could see down between the buildings and it was like a dead spruce stump that wood ants have carved out. Then we landed at LaGuardia Airport.

Everybody was in a hurry at LaGuardia and voices

from the loudspeaker were brash and insistent. People around us were shouting while we waited for our bags and suitcases. We carried them outside to where a sign said the bus to Grand Central Station stopped. It did.

We rode into New York City past a cemetery which was the only open land we saw. It was not really open because it was covered with tombstones. We liked it because we could see that the ground was hilly and not level. The tombstones were grey but they were whiter than the black-red buildings and smokey steel of the trestles and bridges.

When the bus was on the bridge we could see Manhattan, where tall buildings punched the skyline. We could see the Empire State Building, which I knew was near Grand Central Station, where we were going. Everywhere we went people were going. Even when they were there they were going. We too were going because everyone in America is going.

*   *   *

We took a taxicab to Ten Park Avenue. We were staying there with Dan and Eva who were from Palo Alto, California. They had recently moved to New York. Here, Dan called himself Felix, which was also his name, but I had called him Dan for twenty-five years so it was strange that he used his other name in New York. In America names do not often change when other things change. His name was not strange. Only his living in New York on Park Avenue was strange.

When we paid for the cab, we had to put the money in a little drawer through a plastic shield between us and the driver. This was interesting because all the taxicabs we took in New York had this bulletproof shield. When I asked the driver if he thought we might shoot him if he didn't have it he said, "You never can tell."

And although we smiled while we took our bags out

of the taxicab, he did not. He never got out of his seat. Even at Ten Park Avenue he did not get out.

*　　*　　*

We lectured in Plandome which was actually Port Washington. It was not like Manhattan because there were no tall buildings. Mostly there were houses where people live who work in the tall buildings in Manhattan. We stayed overnight with Harold and Shirley. Harold had lived in Alaska and he showed pictures of Kotzebue when he was a small boy there. We talked about Alaska and stayed up too late for me to get up and play tennis with him. Harold played tennis before breakfast because he was keeping in shape. Nearly everyone we talked to was keeping in shape which was interesting because at Koviashuvik we don't care about our shape. Whatever shape we have is the one we have. We do not worry about keeping it.

*　　*　　*

On the train back to Manhattan, the conductor punched holes in our tickets. The holes were in unique shapes. We wanted to keep our tickets but they were taken away from us. Many things in America are taken away, but not really taken away, because we were given a ride on the train for the tickets. The Indians were given glass beads for the island of Manhattan.

*　　*　　*

At Central Park we visited the zoo with Kim. Kim is Billie's son and is a musician. He lived in New York because he knows how to live in New York like we know how to live in the wilderness. We visited the zoo to see grizzly bears but they did not act or look like grizzly bears do in the wilderness. The people at the zoo were like the bears. They did not act or look like people act or look in the wilderness either, but we liked them and we liked the grizzly bears.

*   *   *

Harper and Row is a building full of people who publish books. They had published Billie's book, *Four Seasons North,* and a reporter was there to interview us for the Associated Press. She asked us how we got along together in the wilderness and if Billie felt discrimination because she was a female. The reporter looked at me when she asked the question. Everyone we talked with at Harper and Row was female, and since I was not a female, I felt it best not to say anything and I did not.

Then Billie was interviewed on the radio for the Martha Deane Show. She was asked about the trans-Alaska pipeline which was then being built across Alaska. She said she thought the wilderness was more important. This was not a popular point of view.

Everywhere we went people asked us about the trans-Alaska pipeline. They asked if we were for it or against it. This was not the right question because we were not for or against the pipeline. We said that what little wilderness was left in America was so important that if we do not save it we may not save ourselves.

*   *   *

In New York we were told that the Amtrak train to Boston was a good way to get there and see the country. Mostly we saw dirty factory buildings, warehouses and cemeteries of junk cars.

Outside of Providence, Rhode Island the engine blew a gasket and we were two hours late. We found it interesting because the train was full of people we could watch. Some of them complained about how things do not work like they should, and how nobody expected things to work like they should. After we left Providence we could see some of the country with trees, hills, farms and towns with steeples.

*   *   *

In Boston we did not stay in Boston but went to Harvard with friends. Harvard is not Harvard University, which is in Cambridge. Harvard is a town. Even there, we did not stay in Harvard because our friend's house was in Bolton, which is next to Harvard. In New England nearly everybody lives somewhere else because everyone works somewhere else. This is very confusing because no one really knows where anyone is.

Anyway, we lectured in Harvard and stayed in Bolton with David and Prudence and their baby Andrew. Andrew reminded us of Koviashuvik. Every child we met in America reminded us of Koviashuvik because children make a time and place of joyfulness.

*   *   *

Although we did not stay in Boston, we lectured in Boston. We spoke in Winchester, Worcester, Wellesley Hills, Franklin, Waltham, Sherborn and Lexington, where we met with a special forum of the Boston Industrial Mission. They had our topic listed as "The Other Side of the Alaskan Pipeline," which was interesting to us since we did not know what was on this side of the Alaskan pipeline. We were told that a representative of the oil industry had addressed the Boston Industrial Mission on "This Side of the Pipeline," so we talked about the other side of the pipeline. We assumed "the other side of the Alaskan Pipeline" to be the northern wilderness, so we talked about the need to protect the wilderness.

In Lexington we enjoyed visiting the Village Green where the Revolutionary War began. We talked with the Reverend and Mrs. Zoerheide, who were living in the parsonage at the edge of the Green. They told us the parsonage was there before the War of Independence. The Zoerheides told us what had happened there because they were interested in history. Since we too were interested in history, we recalled that the trees, which are now logs in our cabin at Koviashuvik, were growing long before the Revolutionary War began near Boston.

*   *   *

In Boston, the golden dome of the State House was like the dome of the capitol of California in Sacramento. Otherwise, Boston was different from Sacramento, Phoenix, Anchorage or Los Angeles because the streets in Boston did not meet at right angles to form squares. However, in Boston, like other cities we visited in America, people were afraid to go out at night and the Arlington Street Church had to lock its doors as soon as the Sunday service was over because the brass pipes in the washroom had been cut out several times. You could sell brass for drugs.

There were hearings in Boston on hand gun control. A woman we heard testify was from Bolton, the town in which we were staying. She had shot someone who had forced his way into her home. She said she did not want to be without protection. We met people everywhere in America who had purchased hand guns. We were asked about the guns we have at Koviashuvik. We said they are rifles. We consider rifles tools and do not own hand guns.

We ate oysters and scrod at Durgin Park Restaurant in Boston. It had been over twenty years since I was there. The city around it was different because of redevelopment. Every city we visited was being redeveloped. No one seemed to think they were being improved.

When we talked at the Unitarian Universalist headquarters, next to the State House on Beacon Hill, people came with backpacks, long hair and two airedales. This was strange because it was the weekly chapel for the staff. The people who had arranged our visit thought we had invited the strangers. We would have invited them but we did not know who they were. We learned

later that they came because an underground newspaper
had listed us as an event. For Billie and me the visiting
airedales were an event. Everywhere we went in New
England we saw airedales but only in Boston did airedales
come to see us.

*   *   *

After we returned to Koviashuvik from our visit to
America, it did not seem like we had been gone except
that the sun had returned and we had to snowshoe new
trails and a wolverine had eaten the fox pelt which was
on a stretch board in front of the cabin.

Billie and I thought about what people said and what
we talked about. We talked mostly about values because
that is what we went outside to talk about. We thought
about how people spoke of values being gone and their
sense of nostalgia for past times. How people are doing
their job and going to school because they do not know
what else to do because everything seems too much of
a mess to do anything about. And how it is not possible
to change anything anyway.

There were some who were excited about what they
were doing and we were excited about what they were
doing. We liked the way their eyes shone and how they
smiled. There were others in America who seemed uneasy, as if they felt they would like to do something or
be something, but they did not know what it was they
wanted to do or be.

It was a strange experience to visit the United States
when you are living in the United States but not really
in the United States, because people in America did not
think of us as really being in the United States. But we
are. Yes, we really are.

To know that you do not know is
the best. To pretend to know when
you do not know is a disease.

LAO TZU

7
Haul Road Hard Hat
What is learned on the way to Bettles

Koviashuvik Creek glittered in the morning sun as I
hoisted my pack and adjusted the shoulder straps. It was
a ten hour hike, across two mountain passes, to the trans-
Alaska pipeline haul road near the village of Wiseman.

No float plane had landed on our lake, as we had
hoped, to shuttle hunters into the higher isolated peaks
of the Brooks Range. Hunting season had begun on the
previous weekend. We had important mail to fly out.
With no passing visitor, I had given myself a deadline of
this Monday morning to start my trek over the mountains.

*　　*　　*

I planned to hitch a ride on the trans-Alaska pipeline
haul road to one of the construction camps along the
route. I was going to a construction camp because each
camp was served by daily flights to Fairbanks. I thought

it would be simple to buy plane fare to Fairbanks and from there fly back to the village of Bettles.

I was wrong.

* * *

My goal was Bettles, our post office and communication center. However, I could not get to Bettles without going to Fairbanks. I was trying to get to the small settlement of Bettles, only eighty miles south-west of us. The bush plane service, upon which we were dependent for our monthly airdrop of mail, was stationed there.

Travel can be complicated. The only way I could get to Bettles without hiking for a week over craggy mountains and marshy, mosquito-plagued tundra was to fly two hundred miles south to Fairbanks and then take another plane back north of the Arctic Circle to Bettles.

To get eighty miles from home, I had to go five hundred miles and visit a city I did not want to visit and meet people I did not know. I did not want to meet some of the people I met or go where I had to go but it is no longer possible to get where you want to go without going somewhere else and meeting people you don't know.

* * *

Anyway, at eight o'clock in the morning on August eleventh, I kissed Billie good-bye, which is different from kissing her hello. After kissing her good-bye, I started up the steep slope behind our shore camp.

Fox sparrows flitted from willow bush to spruce trees and back to willow. They flew back and forth with me on my climb but did not rest when I stopped near the crest to look back. The lake, below me, reflected the mountains like a broken mirror as breezes ruffled scattered patches of water on its surface. Only the faint rise and fall of the voices of Koviashuvik Creek tumbling below me broke the silence.

The voices of Koviashuvik Creek could be heard like the voices of children on a playground when voices are heard but not the words. Everywhere voices can be heard but not the words.

Soon it was nine o'clock, and I was two thousand feet above our lake. There I could look out across the wide valley of Glacier Creek to Mount Poss. I was up where Mount Poss was thrusting its black jagged peaks into a cobalt sky. We were there with no words. The mountain's voice was there and I heard it.

*   *   *

Through waist-high alders and dense willows, I picked my way down to timber line. It was good walking among the white spruce trees on the soft tundra. The matting of moss and lichens accepted my feet like gifts.

As I reached the brown, iron-stained boulders of Glacier Creek, a sharp-shinned hawk soared into the trees. I jumped across the riffles to a low, flat rock on the other side. There, taking off my backpack and jacket, I dipped my hands in the clear, icy water to splash on my face. The sun on my back was a blessing.

Stretching out on my stomach across the large sun-warmed boulder, I sipped the cold liquid and drifted down among the shining pebbles scoured into jewels by thousands of years of running water. I was not totally among the pebbles because I could still feel the warm rock under my stomach and the sun still caressed my back. Even so, I was down among the jewels, ten thousand years ago, I was there among the jewels.

*   *   *

The roaring thunder of a great Hercules aircraft tore me from the past. Its engines filled the valley as the metal monster cleared the ridge above me by a few hundred feet. It appeared to barely clear the ridge, and its reverberation continued after the plane disappeared to the north behind Sukakpak Mountain. As the sound diminished, I stood up and again hoisted my pack, recalling why I had not wanted to make this trip.

We had learned from a recent mail drop that the bush air service in Bettles had been sold. Not only did we not know the new owners, but we did not know if our sole contact with the outside was to continue.

It is a disturbing thing not to know. When you want to know it is disturbing not to know. Even though there are some things we do not want to know, like what our children taste like boiled. I think it was George Bernard Shaw who said that, but Billie and I had supplies at Bettles and we wanted to know.

So, I accepted this trip as inevitable and decided to make the best use of it by taking care of business in Fairbanks on the way to Bettles. I was also curious about what was happening on the trans-Alaska pipeline project then under construction.

From our radio, we knew that the construction road across the Brooks Range had been completed. We had heard on the radio that work had begun on the pipeline itself.

All summer we had been reminded of the giant project by the low-flying cargo aircraft which sometimes shifted their course from the pipeline corridor air route to detour over our isolated lake. They flew low over the lake, apparently sightseeing, on their way to the construction camps to the north.

*   *   *

I too was sightseeing as I climbed over the top of Sukakpak Ridge just north of Battlement Rock. I was seeing sights in the open swale below the out-jutting cliffs.

One of the sights was a grizzly bear, feeding on cloud-berries, about four hundred yards beyond me. Its light, golden shoulders blended into the brown of its rump as it moved among the sedge tussocks. It did not see me. It was not sightseeing.

This might be a sow with cubs. Carefully, I scanned the open ridge for other bears. I was unarmed. I did not want to encounter a female grizzly with cubs where there was no tree to climb.

Once a visiting hunter asked me what to do if attacked by a grizzly with cubs, north of timber line.

I said, "Climb a tree."

"But there are no trees beyond timber line," he said.

"You had better climb one anyway," I said.

Where I was sightseeing, there was no tree to climb and a sow with cubs could be a concern. Even though I saw no bear cubs, I carefully picked my way across the tussocks and moved down the steep slope to the trees near the headwaters of Gold Creek. There I stopped to eat. Billie had put in my pack a gourmet's delight of golden fried snowshoe hare and sourdough cookies. The difference between a repast and a feast has little to do with quantity. With a cup of the clear rushing water from Gold Creek, my lunch was a feast.

*   *   *

Placer gold was discovered on this creek in 1900, which is why it is called Gold Creek. Prospectors panned for gold throughout the six mile length of the creek to where it ended at the Middle Fork of the Koyokuk River.

Marking my trail down Gold Creek canyon were rusty barrels, disintegrating cabins and occasional remains of the old wagon road from the village of Wiseman. To me they were ghosts of a dream of riches in the past. The dreams go on. Today it is oil that feeds the dream in

Alaska. Greed for the fast buck again brings the same ruthless invasion of this northern wilderness.

Scrambling up from the creek, I found a wagon that had been abandoned years ago after the road washed out. It still had much of its original paint. Readable on the sideboard was "Webber—Since 1845." It had apparently been abandoned shortly after it was brought here because there was little wear on the iron tires. It was probably shipped by steamboat up the Yukon River and pulled on a barge by horses as far as possible up the Middle Fork of the Koyokuk River. Finally, it arrived at the village of Wiseman before being hitched to horses and hauled to Gold Creek.

Now the wagon was being recycled as a roost for spruce grouse and a shelter for wolves. There were droppings in the wagon and urine stains on the wagon wheels.

*   *   *

In the late afternoon, I climbed out of the canyon and started down a marshy slope to the Middle Fork of the Koyokuk River. As Hakim Sani said, "When you get to the river you do not talk about the tributary."

From two miles away, while walking down the marshy slope, I heard the grating sound. Long before I saw its cause, I heard the rumble of machinery drifting up from the scar of a huge gravel pit.

Gone was the silence of the mountains and valleys I had left. By the time I reached the pipeline project haul road, I could separate the clatter of earth movers from the occasional helicopter and the roar of trucks as they hurled past me with their loads of pipe and equipment.

I stood on a shoulder of the gravel highway six feet above the soft tundra in a cloud of dust. High above the soft tundra, I stood on the edge of the gravel and held out my thumb. With my pack on my back, I kept my thumb extended as the next five trucks' backwash of air and flying gravel buffeted me. The trucks never paused. One driver waved. I turned and hiked down the hard shoulder of this alien gravel platform toward the village of Wiseman.

*　　*　　*

There is not much left of Wiseman. Today there are not many people living in Wiseman like there were when Robert Marshall wrote a book about Wiseman in the 1930s. He called it *Arctic Village*, but the community was called Wiseman when he wrote the book. It is still confusing because today Arctic Village is an Indian community in the Brooks Range with a zip code 99723. Arctic Village has a zip code today but not Wiseman.

Wiseman Creek runs into the Middle Fork of the Koyokuk River as it did in 1901 when Wright's Roadhouse was the only building and the creek was being panned for gold. It was first panned for gold in 1901. By 1915 Wiseman was a village serving three hundred whites and a hundred natives in the area. Today only a handful of people live permanently in Wiseman.

The most interesting thing about Wiseman today is a continuing feud, the start of which no one remembers. Like nations of people who can't cooperate, Wiseman is isolated. It has even isolated itself from the trans-Alaska pipeline haul road, which passes the village on the far side of the Middle Fork of the Koyokuk River.

*　　*　　*

As I hiked along the haul road, a yellow pickup slowed to a stop beside me. I looked through the open window to the driver who had the name DON AUVERSON painted in large letters on his hard hat. He said he could give me a lift a mile or so down the road.

I threw my pack into the truck bed and climbed up

on the dusty, plastic seat. As we moved along, Don asked me where I was going and at what camp I worked.

When he learned that Billie and I lived in the range over a couple of ridges from the river he asked, "Is your name Wright? I've heard of you. You wrote a book didn't you?"

I said it was probably my wife's book, her journal of our first year in the wilderness before the oil strike at Prudhoe Bay started the trans-Alaska pipeline project. Then it was my turn to learn about him.

He was from Idaho and called himself an equipment engineer. He was stationed at Dietrich pipeline camp to the north of us and his contractor only worked as far south as Minnie Creek. He said he could only take me that far because south of Minnie Creek a different con-tractor worked north out of Coldfoot camp. It was strange to hear him speak of Minnie Creek. I knew it as a creek with high-finned, iridescent grayling darting from riffle to rock. Now it was just a boundary. To Don Auverson it was just this boundary between contractors.

Don had been in Alaska only a few weeks and he asked many questions about the winter cold. I said it would not be too different from what he knew in northern Idaho. When I said that, I had never spent a winter in northern Idaho. Now that I have been in northern Idaho in the winter, I don't think I would say that again. I prefer our winters in the Arctic.

Anyway, Don was interested in the way Billie and I lived isolated in a cabin we had built ourselves with simple hand tools. He said it was like his childhood, and he would like to try living that way again.

"Except, I have a daughter in high school," he said, "And I've been out of debt for ten years."

His voice was drowned out by the roar of a diesel truck.

The pickup swayed in the turbulence as a huge load of pipe hurled past.

I wondered what being out of debt ten years had to do with living like we do in the wilderness. I did not ask. We slowed to a stop on a wide spot near Minnie Creek and he said, "This is as far as I go. Do you mind if I take your picture?"

I shouldered my pack and posed. I do not like to pose but when we are self-conscious we pose. I posed and then we shook hands.

"Stick out your thumb," he said. "You should have no trouble getting a ride."

*   *   *

I stuck out my thumb each time a truck went by. I stuck out my thumb until seven-thirty. I had crossed the Middle Fork of the Koyokuk and the Hammond rivers on their new bridges without getting a ride. I was thankful that I did not have to wade and swim the icy rivers, as was necessary the year before. Still, I regretted the bridges. I regretted that the solitude of the valley was now gone forever. Because of the bridges, gone forever.

*   *   *

Hiking into the spruce trees, about three hundred yards from the haul road, I pitched my small tent. Lying in my sleeping bag, I listened to the Doppler effect of approaching and receding trucks. There were no familiar night sounds of the wilderness. Only the sound of trucks. Approaching and receding trucks.

Finally I fell asleep.

*   *   *

And I dreamed.

In the dream I was crossing the San Francisco Bay Bridge on a Sunday morning, as I had in the early nineteen sixties. I was driving Victor Frankl from Berkeley to the First Unitarian Church in San Francisco where he was to speak.

I had arranged his speaking engagements in the Bay Area. I had arranged for him to speak at the University of California, at Napa State Hospital and Langley Porter Clinic because he was founder of the Vienna School of Logotherapy and had written *From Death Camp to Existentialism*. People wanted to hear him talk because he had been a prisoner in a Nazi death camp. That is why they wanted to hear him. Mostly because he had been in a death camp and survived.

Anyway, as we drove across the bridge we talked about solitude and how solitude is not loneliness. We talked about solitude but not in the dream. In the dream we did not talk. In the dream we drove between bulldozers and trucks. We could not talk because the machines made too much noise. We just nodded to each other because we shared a knowledge about death camps and mountain wilderness as we drove into the Treasure Island tunnel. Coming out of the tunnel, in the dream, I could see an arctic sky ahead.

I opened my eyes and it was dawn.

*   *   *

By seven o'clock I had flapped the ice from the tent fly and repacked my gear. Then, scrambling down the bank of the Middle Fork of the Koyokuk, I washed the sleep from my eyes.

I had hiked two miles down the haul road while trucks roared past my outstretched thumb. A station wagon stopped. In it were a man and woman wearing hard hats. They picked me up. They said they were employed at Dietrich Camp and were driving to Coldfoot Camp on business. They asked me at which camp I worked.

After explaining who I was, we talked about Billie's

and my life in the range. I learned that they had been in Alaska only a short time. She for a month, he two weeks. They were here for the money. They said, "For the money."

Later, Billie and I went to work on the trans-Alaska pipeline project for money. We were counselors in construction camps north of the Yukon. There had never before been counselors in construction camps the way we were counselors. However, that was later on. Now I was at Coldfoot Camp for the first time.

*　　*　　*

At Coldfoot Camp I found the office of Green Associates, the general contractor for this section of the project, and inquired about the possibility of catching a ride to Fairbanks. I was referred to a gray-haired man in an aluminum hard hat who seemed to be in authority.

"Were you fired or are you leaving for R and R?" he asked.

I assumed that R and R meant rest and recreation, but it was confusing to both of us as I tried to explain my situation. He suggested that I go to the entrance of the camp at the haul road. "You'll have no trouble getting a ride," he said. "You might be questioned at the Yukon River crossing when you get on the hovercraft, but I don't think you will have any problem. It is the only thing I can suggest."

Just then another man in a hard hat came in, and ignoring me, nodded to the man with whom I was speaking. They both disappeared into an inner office.

I walked out to the haul road at the camp entrance and again raised my thumb.

*　　*　　*

A station wagon with three young men in their blue, plastic hard hats pulled up beside me and the door swung open.

When I climbed in, one of them asked, "Where 'ya goin'?"

I said, "Fairbanks, but actually I am on my way to Bettles. It's just that I can't get there from here."

"We're not going that far," the driver said. "We're not even going as far as Prospect Camp, but you can probably catch a truck when we stop."

"You on R and R?" asked another. Again I explained that I lived in the range.

"Sounds great! Will you have some donuts?" the front seat passenger asked. He passed a paper bag back to me.

"You ought to catch one of those trucks. It'll take you directly into Fairbanks," my companion in the back seat said as he reached into the donut bag. The donut left sugar on his black mustache and beard.

"Wouldn't they stop for you?" he asked.

I told them about my experience as a trans-Alaska pipeline haul road hitch-hiker.

"What you need is a hard-hat," my back-seat companion said. "Yeah, you need a hard hat like this one here on the floor, if I can get the damned lining to work."

He picked up a red, plastic hard hat from among the tools on the floor of the wagon and began working with the inner straps.

"You are nobody on this project without a hard hat," he said.

"You are nobody on this project, period," said the man in the front seat.

"Unless you are from Texas," said the driver.

"Don't take us too seriously," said the man next to me as he struggled with the straps in the plastic hard hat. "No, don't take us too seriously. We're just pissed off with Texans that's all. We feel we've been invaded."

He handed me the hat and said, "There y'are. Try that on."

With a red, plastic hard hat on my head, I felt I belonged. Yes, all it took was a hard hat. It is strange that all it took was a red, plastic hard hat.

*   *   *

The station wagon turned off the haul road to the pipeline work pad. I got out and thanked my hosts for the ride and donuts.

Squaring the red plastic hard hat on my head, I hiked to a place on the side of the road wide enough for a vehicle to pull off and put my pack down beside me.

The first vehicle stopped. It was a pickup truck. I threw my pack in the back and climbed in.

The driver and passenger both looked native. Stenciled on the driver's hard hat was the name FRANK OKEASIK. I thought he might be from Nome. Okeasik is an Eskimo name from Nome. He was.

*   *   *

Frank asked me what work I was doing on the pipeline project and when I told him that I lived here in the mountains he said, "I see you are wearing a hard hat."

I told him it was to get a ride and laughed.

"It sure worked," he said.

Okeasik said he was an oiler. His partner never spoke. He just smiled.

Frank drove me into Prospect Camp to the Green Associates Construction trailer module where the Wien Alaska Airlines agent had an office. When I went in no agent was there.

However, I was greeted by a friendly native Alaskan who said he was working as an accountant for Green Associates. He said his name was Chuck Evan and he offered me a cup of hot coffee and a sweet roll. He told me that I had just missed the morning's flight to Fairbanks and that the agent was still out at the airstrip. He told me there would be another flight in the afternoon.

When he learned how Billie and I lived alone in the range, our talk became tribal. I say tribal because Chuck was an Eskimo who had grown up north of the Yukon. After I told him Frank Okeasik had picked me up, we found we had mutual acquaintances in northern Alaskan villages.

*   *   *

When the airline agent arrived, I asked about a reservation on the next flight to Fairbanks.

"Fine," he said and took out a form and poised his pencil. "Reason for going?"

"To get to Fairbanks," I said.

"O.K., but what's the reason?" he said. "I've got to put it down here." He looked directly at me for the first time. "Were you fired? Are you sick, or on R and R? What is your number?"

After I convinced him that I was not part of the pipeline project and that I was a resident of the area he seemed perplexed. He was perplexed because he said, "I don't know if you can fly if you are a resident. I don't think you can fly."

I asked him what the fare was to Fairbanks. He said he did not know but would look it up and he did.

"It is forty-two dollars and sixty-four cents."

I asked if I could give him a check and he looked relieved. He said he was relieved because he couldn't handle cash. Since I had no number and was not employed by the pipeline project, he did not know the procedures. Besides, he had only been on the job for two weeks. He said he would put me on the afternoon flight and would act ignorant about it if my passage was not permissible.

"If you want a receipt," he said, "go to the airline desk in Fairbanks and tell them you came in from here and want a receipt."

I said my cancelled check would be enough.

*   *   *

During the five hours I waited for my flight, I heard many conversations, and I read. I am a compulsive reader. I read everything I see. I read all the notices posted on the walls.

The largest notice was painted on a three foot plaque at the entrance of the office module and the word NOTICE was printed in large white, capital letters on a black background. The rest of the sign, in black letters on a white background, read:

> Fornicating, searching, camping, hunting, fishing, trapping and shooting within the right of way is prohibited. All employees from Alyeska Pipeline Service Co., its agents, contractors or sub-contractors and their employees are affected by this stipulation. — Federal-State Stipulation Section 1-4 Alyeska Pipeline Service Co.

On a closer inspection, I saw that the words fornicating and searching had been added with a felt pen to match the original stenciling.

The agent said there had been controversy over searching for liquor before the "no liquor" rule had been rescinded. I asked if liquor had become a problem and he said, "I don't think it has made much difference. I don't see any more drunks than before. Maybe even less."

A bull-cook (the term used for employees who worked cleaning rooms and in the kitchen) told me that fornicating alluded to some of the many women employed on the project.

"Some of them are doubling their wages on their back," he said. "I can understand them getting a better job placement that way but it's not fair to the decent gals."

Among the many notices posted was the movie and TV schedule. I was told that television tapes came from

Fairbanks broadcasts two weeks after the original broadcasts outside Alaska. [Today satellites bring direct television to Eskimo and Indian villages so they can see reruns and Miss America finals direct from Atlantic City, Las Vegas or Albuquerque. The haul road is now a gravel highway through the wilderness and prostitutes no longer need to be imported.]

*   *   *

During my five hours in Prospect Camp, I was reminded of a military operation. I discussed this with a culinary worker who said, "It's like an enlightened prison."

"What do you mean?" I asked.

"Well," he said, "It's like a prison where the only difference is you can make good money and you can quit, but there is no day off, and if you take it before your R and R you're fired. I know because I've spent time and they furnish you with just about everything except freedom."

"What is freedom?" I asked, and he showed me the palms of his hands and shrugged his shoulders.

"Yeah," another said, "I've never had it so good. Great food, good quarters and have you seen all that stuff in the recreation room?"

"Yeah," said another, "Guys complain anyway. I guess it's human nature."

So I visited the recreation room with its pool tables, chessboards and gymnastic equipment. There were magazines and a popcorn machine in the trailer module, even a sauna. Yes, an electrified sauna that heated artificial rocks north of the Arctic Circle.

There was nothing artificial about the three telephone booths next to the sauna, however. They were real. Each had a sign on the door which said there were two more "morale phones" located at the movie hall. I learned that, from these booths, anyone could call collect to any place in the nation. Next to the phone booths there was a sign over a door which read NATIVE COUNSELOR.

Later on I was going to be a native counselor in pipeline camps north of the Yukon as well as a general site-counselor for anyone on the pipeline project. But at this time I did not know that within a year Billie and I would both be camp counselors, or that Prospect would be one of her camps.

*   *   *

Well, I flew from Prospect Camp into Fairbanks and caught the bi-weekly flight back to Bettles. I finally got to Bettles but it wasn't easy. It was interesting but it wasn't easy.

In Bettles I chartered the small float plane, moored to the bank of the Koyokuk River, for the eighty mile flight home.

Crammed in with our supplies and groceries, the pilot circled our cabin at Koviashuvik to let Billie know we were going to set down on the lake.

I waded ashore with the red plastic hard hat on my head. I waded to where Billie was waiting for me and kissed her hello, which was different from kissing her goodbye. Yes, it was.

And that is what I learned on my way to Bettles. Beyond the symbolic importance of wearing a hard hat, I learned that kissing Billie hello is very different from kissing her goodbye.

That is not all I learned, but what is most important is not the easiest to learn, but it is the most important.

> *In all things of nature there is*
> *something of the marvelous.*
> ARISTOTLE, 384-322 B.C.

8
Caribou
The meaning of pattern

The wolves' slashing teeth kept the caribou in a tramped-down ring of blood-stained snow. Each time the caribou made a lunge to escape he was turned back by bared teeth.

It was a drama of desperation. Not pleasant to see. From the snow-drifted hill above the lake, I had watched the wolves pursue this pacing caribou, separating him from the migrating herd.

After being separated from the herd, the young bull with antlers held high plunged through the drifts on the frozen lake outdistancing the two wolves behind him. Then his escape was cut off by three other wolves. They dashed from the spruce trees on the shore and cut off his escape. One of the wolves had torn the caribou's hind quarter. It was gaping red, but he did not fall.

Now he stood in a blood-stained circle of snow while

the wolves waited for him to weaken. They waited for him to weaken while the migrating herd continued across the white expanse of the lake as if nothing had happened.

*   *   *

The migrating herd of more than a hundred cows, yearlings and a few bull caribou continued on. Like most of us, when something happens, we just continue on.

*   *   *

Earlier the herd of caribou had been lying at rest. They had bedded down in the snow near the center of the lake. Then the presence of the wolves near the shore was sensed by a cow who rose from her bed and started plodding north through the drifts. She broke the trail.

As she started north, several other deer rose to follow her. In single file, nose to tail, they followed her lead up the center of the white plain.

*   *   *

It was then I first saw the wolves. Two gray wolves were bounding through the snow toward the herd. Then the herd bolted and scattered in all directions across the knee-deep snow.

The young bull, separated from the rest, paced toward the trees on shore with the pair of wolves leaping through the snow behind him.

The pacing deer outdistanced the wolves but the wolves kept following him until he was met by three other wolves at the shore. He was cornered when the three wolves in the spruce trees cut off his escape.

In many ways wolves are civilized animals. For this reason some people dislike wolves. Like civilization, wolves know how to cut off escape.

*   *   *

The caribou was injured but his hoofs were still a threat. The wolves appeared in no hurry to finish their prey. The two gray wolves lay panting in the snow while a large black wolf circled the bleeding animal. He was followed by two smaller gray wolves.

The three wolves circled the wounded deer giving him no rest. They continued to circle him, slashing at his hind quarters, until the caribou could no longer defend himself.

To be partially eaten alive is not a pleasant way to die but this is the way we will all go. Whether by disease or cancer or some other way, we will ultimately be eaten. But not by wolves. No, it is not likely that it will be wolves.

*　　　*　　　*

It has been said that nature cares for the species and sacrifices the individual. That the individual is sacrificed because nature cares for the race. From my observation, nature has no care. Nature has necessity but not care. The only thing that can care is an individual. My feeling of care for the young caribou was not because I was an individual because some individuals don't care. But I care.

*　　　*　　　*

Wolves and humans are the primary predators of caribou. Wolves have followed the migrating herds for thousands of years. Our ancestors also followed the caribou herds in Europe and Asia. Today we are still primary predators. We and the inland Nunamiut Eskimos have been dependent upon these arctic deer for centuries.

Not only have caribou meat and fat provided ninety percent of the Nunamiut diet, but their clothing, tents, bindings and ropes were made from caribou skin.

From antlers and bone, they made tools. Even the fuel for their transportation came from caribou. It was the meat of caribou that fed the sled dogs.

I wonder if the oil being pumped from the north slope of the Brooks Range was once caribou.

*   *   *

The warmest clothes are those made from caribou skin. We made our winter mukluks from the hide of a caribou. Dependency on caribou in the Brooks Range of northern Alaska still exists. Even with the replacement of sled dogs by snowmobiles and the availability of mail order goods and tools, caribou is still central in the Eskimo's diet. Without caribou the village of Anaktuvuk Pass would be entirely dependent upon outside sources for food.

In the past, Eskimos starved when the migrations shifted. In the past people ate their dogs when the migrations shifted.

In a technological society there is also hunger. People can still starve in their souls. They eat their hearts out instead of their dogs.

*   *   *

In spring the barren ground caribou migrate north over the mountains from the southern slopes of the Brooks Range. They migrate north from where they spent the coldest months of winter. They travel over the passes in bands of fifty or a hundred and sometimes in a herd of thousands. I watched a herd of more than one thousand caribou cross the lake on their way to the open tundra of the north slope in the spring of 1969.

*   *   *

First, let me tell you about the tundra. Mostly about the tundra flies and mosquitos.

The soggy tundra of the north slope has swarms of mosquitos and nostril flies and warble flies. By July and August warble flies and nostril flies and mosquitos are at their worst. This means they are at their most. When mosquitos and flies are at their most, there is nothing worse for caribou.

In July and August warble flies drill through the caribou's skin to lay their eggs. The larvae form cysts under the hide of the animal's back. In the spring, most caribou are infested with a hundred or more of these larvae. Then, in late spring, the larvae bore through the skin and fall on the tundra leaving a hole in the skin, which makes the hide worthless for the Eskimo.

Anyway, the warble fly needs the caribou to feed its young. I wonder if the caribou needs the warble fly? I don't think so but I wonder. Also I wonder about the nostril flies which infest the animal's nostrils.

In mid summer I watched a caribou stand motionless with its nose thrust down in the moss and lichens. Then, it shook its head and made a wild run across the tundra only to stop suddenly with its nose again thrust into the moss. Then again, it dashed off like I did one summer when I stepped on a wasp nest. I too made a wild dash across the tundra and stopped only when I jumped into a thaw pond.

Caribou will run until nearly exhausted to escape the insect hordes. In their overheated condition they then attract even more of the persistent swarms. This may be why the caribou migrate as far as the arctic coast in search of cool winds to dispel the plague of insects.

I think this is why, but I don't really know because I am not a caribou.

*　　*　　*

I am glad I am not a caribou. Relief from insects comes only with the frosts in late August. Then new ice begins to form in the muskeg. When ice begins to cover the melt ponds on the flats, bands of caribou start south again.

The young bull caribou, which the five wolves brought down on his spring journey north, will miss the flies and mosquitos. He did not miss the wolves.

*　　*　　*

In the same way, Hoyt Glass, who sat in front of me in the eighth grade, missed the last World War and Korea and Vietnam and polio because he was brought down and eaten by bone cancer in the spring of 1934. He was brought down in the spring when he was migrating west with his family. He did not miss bone cancer like the caribou did not miss the wolves.

*   *   *

I like the word caribou. It is an Algonquin Indian word meaning pawer or scratcher. At least the word, caribou, was Algonquin before it was mispronounced by the French.

In Europe, American caribou are called reindeer although they are not. In America, European reindeer are called reindeer but not our caribou. Caribou are not reindeer. Even though they can breed with the European reindeer they are not reindeer. Caribou are not reindeer in the same way wolves are not dogs. Dogs are domesticated.

Caribou and wolves are still wild. People would domesticate them if they could. I hope not, for "In wildness is the preservation of the world," said Thoreau. He was right.

*   *   *

The young bull caribou, whose journeys were now ended, had spent the coldest months of winter with a band of about twenty others in the high open valleys above timber line. There, frequent winds swept the snow to shallow depths making it easier to paw down to lichens than in the more sheltered river valleys.

I had estimated him to be about four years old. I wondered if he had mated for the first time in the fall after his testicles had begun to swell. I wondered if, in that brief breeding cycle of rut in October, he had sparred with older bulls and fathered calves. Young bulls are

often unable to mate until their fifth or sixth year because the stronger, older bulls drive them away from the
cows. After once mating, a bull is said to have courage.

Courage is from the Latin word meaning with heart.
However, this is not affection. With caribou, mating is
not affection. It is nature's necessity. Even the cows,
which come into rut once a year, like the bulls, breed
without affection.

*   *   *

Before rut, bull caribou accumulate a great amount
of fat. They accumulate fat on their backs above the hind
quarters and it is then that they are most hunted by the
Nunamiut Eskimos.

When rut begins, the male caribou stops eating and
lives from his accumulated fat. The meat then has a
strong flavor and it is not pleasant.

I have observed some institutions and people who,
after accumulating enough fat, are not as pleasant as they
were.

Anyway, after rut, when the caribou's stored fat has
been lost, the meat may be tough and stringy but it is
eatable. It is tough but not unpleasant.

*   *   *

There are many theories about the cause of caribou
migration. From a response to hormone secretion, or the
need to drop calves on the tundra, to a reaction to insects. Whatever the cause, all migrations have patterns
and caribou have a migration pattern developed through
years of response to their environment.

*   *   *

The first herd of caribou to migrate through our valley
one spring was seen from the mountain above as a dark
shadow breaking the uniformly white surface of the
frozen lake where the caribou were lying motionless in
the snow.

With my field glasses, I could count fifty-two caribou in the band. I was interested in their pattern of movement, developed through the centuries of travel across these northern mountains.

From the motionless herd, a large female got to her feet and stood looking across the lake as if contemplating the direction in which to go. She stood looking in one direction, then turned her head toward the herd lying bunched together in the snow.

When the old cow arose, several other deer raised their heads but did not get up. They watched the old cow standing there until she started at a plodding walk through the deep snow. Then others began to rise. Soon the whole herd was on its feet. After the cow had plodded away from the group, she stopped about twenty yards beyond and looked back at the huddled animals.

Leaders look back to see if they are being followed. If they are not being followed, they are not leading. Even with caribou it takes following to be a leader.

*   *   *

After the old cow gazed back at the herd, she again plodded ahead. Then a caribou from the herd followed her lead. Then another and another, in single file. Soon all the caribou were strung out in a long, dark line, head to tail, on the white expanse. The lead cow's distance remained a consistent twenty yards ahead of the line.

She was the idea. In the concept of pattern, the old cow was an idea that broke trail through unmarked territory. However, the territory was not totally unmarked because her inner compass pointed north. Instinctively, she knew where she was going. Somehow she knew the direction.

Suddenly the lead cow stopped. Then the other caribou came to a halt as if a signal had run down the line.

After a pause, the old cow made an abrupt right-angle

turn and continued as if she were on her way to the nearer shore. It was as if she were following a new idea.

As for the other caribou, they continued in her track, changing their direction only when they reached the exact place where she made her turn. The dark line of animals was now a moving right angle against the white snow.

Again the lead cow stopped. Then, as if changing her mind, the old cow started off again in the direction she had originally taken, so that a great Z was marked on the white surface of the lake by the moving line of animals.

I saw the pattern as a Z, but it could have been an N if I had been standing someplace else. What one sees depends upon where one stands. Patterns depend upon where one stands.

Anyway, it is interesting that the old caribou made the letter Z, and so did I.

* * *

The lead caribou continued into the spruce trees at the northern end of the lake, and like a string of ants on a familiar path, the herd trailed after her.

All that remained on the white plain of the lake was a single, thin zig-zag line. An idea.

Idea comes from the Greek and Latin meaning form or model. All that remained to mark the snow was an idea of their passing.

* * *

Unlike the old lead cow, which in the late summer wears a small set of antlers, a mature bull in autumn carries a great rack of antlers which sweep back and up, flattening into pointed palms at their ends. Over his brow he carries one, and sometimes two, shovel-like tines which extend out over his square muzzle.

Cows also carry antlers, unlike most deer, and so do

the calves. Calves grow a small spike five or six inches long. Only the bulls have the great sweeping bows. Bulls have massive necks and low hanging white manes which contrast strikingly with their darker faces and legs.

A mature bull can weigh more than 350 pounds. This is less than a moose or an elk, but more than other deer.

* * *

The caribou's hoofs, unlike the dainty hoofs of smaller deer, are large and broad, with soft centers that are rimmed by a tough outer shell. The outer shell makes it possible to keep a footing on slick ice and rocks. The hoof's broad surface also enables the caribou to travel across marshy tundra in summer and the snow in winter. In winter I can easily walk on a caribou trail without snowshoes.

The caribou's hoofs are also shaped for digging down through frozen drifts after moss and lichens. Being slightly concave, their hoofs are adapted for pawing for food. This is why these deer were called scratcher, *exalibu,* by the Algonquin Indians.

Caribou calves are born on the north slope of the Brooks Range in late May or early June. They are born where the cows have scattered across the vast tundra. As soon as the calf is licked dry, it can accompany its mother.

After the frosts have turned the tundra yellow-gold with splashes of red dwarf alder, the calf will follow its mother as she joins the bands of other caribou migrating south across the range to the southern foothills.

* * *

After the long winter night, when a returning sun calls the caribou north again, the calf will travel back over the mountains with its mother and the migrating herd. Even though now weaned, the yearling will stay with its mother until she is ready to give birth again.

*　　*　　*

I like caribou. And this is why I like what our ancestors saw when they drew pictures of caribou on cave walls in France and Spain more than twenty thousand years ago. They drew pattern. From caribou they drew the meaning of life.

Pussy cat, pussy cat
where have you been?
I've been to London
to visit the queen.

Pussy cat, pussy cat
what did you there?
I frightened a mouse
under a chair.

NURSERY RHYME

9
Where is Truth
A visit to the British Museum

We left the twenty-second of January.

It is cold in January at Koviashuvik. It was thirty-five degrees below zero on the Fahrenheit thermometer outside our window.

A returning sun was still not visible above the horizon as we closed our cabin door and sledded our luggage down hill to meet the bush plane. Its engine kept running while we loaded our bags because it was much colder on the lake than up the hill at our cabin. It was too cold on the lake to stop the engine.

Yes, it was colder on the lake. The pilot said it was fifty-five below zero. I checked the plane's thermometer. It was.

*   *   *

After the skis of the small plane lifted from the snow-covered lake, we climbed steeply above the peaks and squinted for the first time in two months at the great fiery ball on the horizon in a southern sky. We squinted at the sun but we smiled at each other as crimson craggs stretched to the north from horizon to horizon while we circled behind the rocky spires of Poss Mountain on our way to London.

*   *   *

Were we really on our way to London to do research in the British Museum I wondered. Or was it to play tourist and ride through Piccadilly Circus on a double-decker bus and read epitaphs in Westminster Abbey or stroll along the Thames and compare British and American inflation. Or was it to visit the Queen?

*   *   *

In the village of Bettles there was no scheduled flight to Fairbanks for three days. However, Daryl, Neil and Carolyn had been expecting us and a great feast was in preparation to greet us. There was moose and lobster tails, roast Dall sheep and prawns. Fresh salad had been flown in and there was good wine and much more.

Debby and Rudy, the school teacher, joined us and after dinner Billie and I shared our film, *North of the Arctic Circle, Human Values and the Land,* before we went to bed.

We went to bed on Neil and Carolyn's couch that pulled out so two people can sleep on it. We went to bed with the roar of the electric-powered oil furnace and the chug of the generator engine next door. We slept on a mattress and springs instead of spruce poles and caribou skins.

*   *   *

Later I got up and the northern lights were dancing outside. Yes, they were still there and the outhouse was still there when I stepped out at forty degrees below zero.

The outhouse was there and the aurora was there and they were both familiar. We all need things familiar.

*   *   *

In the morning Daryl heated the engine of a refurbished crop duster on which skis had replaced wheels and I flew with him to the South Fork of the Koyokuk River to check the thickness of the ice because fuel could be hauled across the ice instead of flying it from Fairbanks. Instead of flying fuel north from Fairbanks there was the possibility of hauling it up the trans-Alaska pipeline project haul road, then across the frozen tundra to supply the generators with which he made light and power for the village of Bettles.

As we swept down to land on the snow-covered river, only the tracks of a passing family of wolves marred the surface. The ice was three feet thick.

Does the River Thames ever freeze?

*   *   *

Then we were in Fairbanks with our adopted family of Syd, Marylou, Katherine, Jessica, Laura, their three cats and two guinea pigs. There we made reservations for a flight to Seattle and Spokane.

The Fairbanks air terminal was overheated at six o'clock in the morning. The cafeteria was crowded with Texas accents, pointed boots, new down parkas and the aroma of crude oil.

After check-in, and the humiliation of a search for hidden weapons, we sat for half an hour with the rest of our fellow travelers all facing the wall of dark glass windows where we watched each other looking back at each other. No one smiled. We had all traded our Fourth Amendment protection against arbitrary search in order to fly.

We were careful not to acknowledge recognition of

one another because we were packaged for transit. We were in transit, being shipped to the British Museum by way of Seattle, Spokane and Seattle.

* * *

We were shipped to Seattle in seats 19D and E. To Spokane in seats 18E and F.

* * *

My adopted brother, Bill, met us at the Spokane airport and we laughed and smiled as he drove us to his home through snow on the outskirts of the city. It was good to get acquainted with his new wife and her two children and I helped nail up sheet rock in the basement.

Billie and I met with a seminar on alternative life styles in Spokane and showed slides and film of Koviashuvik and northern Alaska and talked.

Then we were shipped back to Seattle and put on Pan American's flight 124 to London. We watched a dull movie while flying over Nova Scotia in seats 19F and E.

* * *

It was a long night on the way to London and seat F would not recline. During the only interesting place in the movie the film broke and as we circled Heathrow Airport, just before sunrise, the flight attendant spilled a glass of beer on my head and shoulders while collecting containers from the seats behind us.

The landing was jarring. Something had happened to the plane and it could not taxi to the terminal. A bus was sent out on the wet runway to bring us in to Customs where our passports were stamped and everyone spoke British and I smelled of stale beer.

* * *

While smelling of stale beer in Heathrow Airport, I bought some English money. It was not an exchange, it was a purchase. There is a difference between an exchange and a purchase. An exchange is one thing and a purchase another.

*   *   *

Then we hauled our bags to the top of a two-decker bus and were on our way to London.

In the rain, we were on our way to London through the English countryside high above the morning traffic on the lefthand side of the road atop a red two-decker.

Through the black, bare elms how green the meadows. How sturdy the brick houses with many-paned windows and red-tiled, mottled slate roofs with their stacks of chimney pots.

Then there was the muddy Thames River with houseboats tied against the bank. A river no wider than our Koyokuk River in August high water.

If the Koyokuk were called the Thames would it be the same river? I think so. But if the Thames were called the Koyokuk it would be different. It would be different because it would then have Albert Bridge, named for Prince Albert, whom we knew because his bearded face and bald head looks solemnly at us from the can of tobacco on our cabin table at Koviashuvik.

Anyway, we were now in London at Victoria Station where we could take the tube as close as possible to the British Museum.

*   *   *

A tunnel is a tube in London.

With a two-shilling and a ten-pence piece, which are larger than quarters but smaller than fifty cents, inserted into a slot machine we bought tickets for the underground tube trip to Tottenham Court Road near the British Museum.

English money is funny. To get coins I changed a one pound note worth two dollars and thirty-seven and six-tenths cents and received a seven-sided fifty-pence piece, two ten-pence pieces and two-shilling pieces, a shilling, four pence and two half-pennies. This was an exchange, not a purchase.

*   *   *

Then, with our shoulders pulled down by our bags, we squeezed down stairs and into the tube and onto a train in the morning rush hour. There I thanked the British god that London's underground train routes were coded by color and then thanked our own that we were not color blind.

We got off the Blue line at Oxford Circle and raced with the crowd through tunnels and down stairs to the Orange line, and finally up an escalator and stairs to Tottenham Court Road where we emerged into wind, rain, and a ten-foot sign on a theatre marquee spelling out, THAT'S ENTERTAINMENT. Printed parenthetically beneath: And Do We Need It Now!

Hiking two blocks with four bags in a blowing London rain in early February is not entertainment. A performance perhaps but not entertainment.

*   *   *

Then we were at the Gresham Hotel in Bloomsbury which has been serving the public for two hundred and fifty years with its back to the British Museum.

It accepted us northern Alaskans into a twelve-foot ceiling room with an eight-foot window looking out through the limbs of what appeared to be a great bare beech tree onto a west wing of the Egyptian gallery.

We paused long enough to investigate the toilet down the hall with its long chain-pull and rush of water from an overhead tank, then walked out around the corner along the high iron fence, to the front of the museum's massive building with its great Ionic colonnade. Up the granite steps we hiked to where a guard checked Billie's handbag for explosives.

Pushing through the heavy revolving door we stepped onto the marble floor of the world's greatest treasure house.

*   *   *

We were really there!

We did not stay long. We would have more time in the days to follow. Yet it was somehow necessary to confirm the reality that we were finally here where the colossal red granite head of Thuthmosis the Third from Karnak looked down from the landing above us.

We turned left to the lower Egyptian gallery which housed the famous Rosetta stone, surrendered by Napoleon to the British as a result of Nelson's victory at the Battle of the Nile and the Treaty of Alexandria in 1801.

There it was. Yes, there was the black Rosetta Stone with its message inscribed in hieroglyphs, demonic and Greek, the key that unlocked the language of the ancient Egyptians. I touched it.

*   *   *

On our way out through another gallery, we glanced at handwritten letters with their autographs by Milton, Johnson, Swift, Darwin and hand-scored music by Bach and Beethoven, as well as a sheet from Handel's *Messiah*. They were real!

There they were in the original ink, dipped by those who gave us our heritage, and the intensity of their presence was so great that we headed for the open air where pigeons flew behind the great colonnade outside the museum.

*   *   *

We sat on a bench where we could see across Russell Street. Above the chimney pots on the old brick buildings a gray sky broke to show a glimpse of a familiar arctic blue.

I recalled the snow-capped peaks above our cabin, and the great valley of the Yukon, as we flew south to Fairbanks.

Then we walked down New Oxford Street for tea.

*   *   *

In the old hotel in Bloomsbury where we stayed, people were from all over the world, at least from some place else.

The evening desk clerk was an East Indian and the manager's French accent was as marked as those of the Yugoslavians and Germans who registered the day we arrived.

In the evening Billie and I would go with others to the telly room to hear the BBC news and watch English color television. We sat with those who came from some place else, like the lady from Australia who made it clear that her preference was light entertainment and not the news.

We were not all aliens. There was one somber Englishman who apparently had permanent residence in the hotel. He sat in the same seat each evening and no one else sat there. He made it clear that it was his place, and whenever possible would switch the television station to sportscasts of cricket or soccer scores or to American re-runs. He would turn off the news that we tried to watch so he could see "Mission Impossible."

The underlying theme of British television was our interest. It was evident. Yes, the underlying theme from the colorful thirty-inch screen was unrest and inflation but keep jolly. That was the theme. Billie and I found the viewers and their comments and reactions as interesting as British television. Except for the lady from Australia, they were not interested in sports and entertainment. They came for the news.

*   *   *

We went to bed in a room where visitors to London and the British Museum looked out of this same window at clouds scudding across the stars when America was a colonial outpost and the forebears of our Eskimo neighbors had never seen a white person.

*   *   *

London is an old city. London was old before it was British. Before the Romans occupied the British Isles, there was a community here. There was also a community of Eskimos on Point Hope in northern Alaska before the Romans occupied the British Isles.

There are no double-decker busses in Point Hope, Alaska. We saw no sled-dogs in London. But there was much to see outside the British Museum and we saw what tourists usually see.

*   *   *

Tourists who visit the wilderness of the Brooks Range see what tourists usually see, but seeing is more than looking. Yes, it is. In London we saw huge signs on buildings around Piccadilly Circus——VOLKSWAGEN——SEX SHOP——CINZANO——LONDON PAVILLION.

We also saw the Houses of Parliament, Lambeth Bridge, the Palace and Saint Paul's. We saw Trafalgar Square, Downing Street and Hyde Park. There a man in a raincoat was shouting from atop a small box to an audience of six people in front of two bobbies with hands behind their backs.

In Westminster we walked on ancient graves and at Tottenham Court and Piccadilly Circus we saw hard core pornography displayed larger than life under a giant sign that spelled out SEX CRAFT. In an open court near the Tower of London we watched a crowd gather around a man wrapped in canvas and tied with chains while his partner skillfully conned the crowd into filling his hat with coins in order to see the rest of the act. We looked at more than we saw. Or, was it the other way around?

Anyway, we had tea in Berkeley Square and booked

a tour through Thomas Cook to visit the eleventh-century cathedral in Winchester and three-thousand-year-old Stonehenge on the Salisbury Plain.

*   *   *

When we arrived at Stonehenge, the great monoliths were conveniently arranged next to the highway with an underpass from the parking lot. The sky was gun-metal gray and a raw wind kept half the tourists in the bus.

I had read several monographs on the ancient pre-Druid civilization and about the people who had hauled these fifty-ton rocks to this spot for what was believed to be mystic rites related to the summer solstice.

At Koviashuvik the sun never drops below the horizon at midsummer. At the winter solstice, Billie and I had cut and hauled a spruce tree to the center of our frozen lake. I told about this earlier. On the shortest day of the year we raised a tree as the earth seemed to stand still before turning back to a new year of sun.

I wonder if we share something with the ancient people of Stonehenge.

*   *   *

Then there was Winchester.

In the old capital of Winchester legend says that King Arthur sat here at the Round Table with his knights in the dark days of dragons and chivalry. The thousand-year-old Norman section of the cathedral was no longer legend to us. It was a symbolic connector. So were the few thatched roofs still cherished by those who are wealthy enough to afford their reproduction today.

The roof of our cabin is tundra. We cannot afford to fly in steel or aluminum.

*   *   *

We were impressed by the British spirit on prominent signs in every village and wherever we went in London. In spite of letter bombs, inflation and economic reces-

sion we read, TAKE COURAGE. Everywhere we saw signs
that said, TAKE COURAGE. Sometimes it was just the word,
COURAGE, over the front of a pub. We discovered that
Courage is the name of a brand of beer sold throughout
England.

Billie and I never took Courage in Britain as we are
not fond of warm beer. But the history of real courage
was everywhere, from bomb-scarred monuments to
Captain Robert Scott's ship *Discovery*, anchored to the
bank of the muddy Thames.

*   *   *

In the captain's cabin on the ship *Discovery*, we were
gently rocked by a passing cruise ship as we relived the
tragic Antarctic expedition.

I read Scott's poignant last penciled entry in his diary
in the British Museum. The paper was turning yellow.

"We shall stick it out to the end but we are getting
weaker of course and the end cannot be far. It seems
a pity but I do not think I can write more."

And then he wrote:

"Last entry—For Gods sake look after our people."

Walking the gangplank back to shore I read the word
"Courage" on a beer carton that had been left on the
bank by the tide.

*   *   *

We never did get to visit the Queen. She had gone
to visit the West Indies where it never snows and iced
rum replaces courage. Anyway, while we were in London
we were mostly in the British Museum.

*   *   *

On our way to Stonehenge, the man who talked about
everything on our Cooks Tour said the British Museum

has the greatest collection of mankind's past in the world. This was the primary reason we came to London. We came because Billie and I are futurists.

Futurists are interested in the past because they cannot know where they are going unless they know where they have been. We have been in the British Museum.

* * *

In the Egyptian Gallery of the British Museum we saw a two-thousand-year-old sarcophagus with its delicately-wrapped mummy encrusted with precious stones. The sarcophagus was carved from the trunk of a cedar of Lebanon, cut by slaves and shipped to Egypt. It was cut and shipped from Lebanon. Today there are no forests of cedars of Lebanon left in Lebanon.

In the courtyard of Salisbury Cathedral, we walked beneath a giant cedar from Lebanon. Its seed was brought to England by Crusaders. Brought back by Crusaders who also brought back Damascus steel.

The gun that killed Alexander Hamilton is reputed to have been made of Damascus steel. My father had a Damascus steel shotgun in New Mexico. I shot my first quail with it. My father told me about the cedars of Lebanon which were cut from the forest to construct King Solomon's Temple in Jerusalem.

Today forests of cedars of Lebanon are only words printed on paper, made from trees cut by chain-saws in southeastern Alaska.

* * *

It is interesting that in the British Museum I thought about Alaska and the small spruce logs from which we built our home, and the modern rifle hanging over our bunk with which we kill for our winter meat. Nothing has really changed. No, even if we extend our cabin to a skyscraper and our rifle to a nuclear bomb.

*   *   *

Now listen to this.

In the Ethnography department, which is not in the British Museum proper because it is in the former Civil Service Building in Burlington Gardens, there were collections made on a voyage of Captain Cook to the Pacific between 1767 and 1780 when Alaska was discovered.

The truth is that Alaska was not discovered by Captain Cook. It was not discovered by Captain Cook because he brought back ivory carvings by people whose ancestors discovered Alaska thousands of years before.

We saw collections made by Admiral Perry's expedition to the Arctic in 1826, and the truth is that these carvings and tools are still being made by me and my neighbors. We are still using the materials at hand. Carving a fish-lure from the plastic of a toothbrush catches fish as well as ivory from the tooth of a walrus or an extinct mammoth.

*   *   *

"If truth is not to be found on the shelves of the British Museum," wrote Virginia Woolf in A *Room of One's Own*, "Where, I asked myself, picking up a notebook and pencil, is truth?"

"I like museums. I like to look out of their windows," wrote Gertrude Stein.

We looked out of the windows of the British Museum at Alaska and ancient Egypt. Through the windows of the British Museum we saw slaves building pyramids and pigeons on the roof across Russell Street and our Eskimo neighbors at Anaktuvuk Pass replacing spark plugs in their snowmobiles. We looked out at the world and saw ourselves looking in.

I am the self that dwells in the heart of every mortal creature; I am the beginning, the life span, and the end of all.

I am death that snatches all; I also am the source of all that shall be born.

I am time without end; I am the sustainer; my face is everywhere.

BHAGAVAD GITA

10
Itigak
Bird of Light

The arctic tern plummeted straight down hitting the water with a splash.

The tern struck the water in the shallow cove of the lake like a falling rock. Then, quickly rising into the air, it hovered above the same spot. Poised with beating wings, the bird dropped again and rose with a small fish in its beak, then continued flying along the open water between melting lake ice and the shore.

We knew this particuar tern from the year before. We called him Itigak.

*　　*　　*

With the first open water at Koviashuvik, the arctic terns arrive. The terns arrive at their nesting site before the ice is gone from the lake. They arrive from the other end of the earth.

Two months earlier this same bird was swooping along

the shelf-ice off the coast of Antarctica. There with other terns he had spent the winter while our lake was locked in the cold of the long night. Above the intense blue of the Antarctic Ocean he dived for food where penguins swam and the emerald ice curved into the sea.

Now he was back in the northern sun to mate and hatch two downy chicks on the shore of Koviashuvik. By the end of the summer they would be able to follow their parents south into the winter light, eleven thousand miles away.

*   *   *

Birds of light.

We call them birds of light because eight months of the year they live in continual daylight.

With their clean-cut beauty of design, their slender wings and body of silver-white beneath a pearl-grey above, they are more streamlined than a gull.

With a head capped in solid black, emphasizing a sharp, crimson beak, they fly with grace, enhanced by long, tapered wings and pointed tail which opens into a deep fork as it sweeps against the sky.

*   *   *

This arctic tern was circling in flight south of the Antarctic Circle over the Bellingshausen Sea when he felt the call of Koviashuvik. Like Billie and I feel the call of Koviashuvik. We too respond to ancient cycles.

I think we respond to something still not too dimmed within the mysterious matrix which composes our bodies. We respond in the spring to the call of Koviashuvik like the arctic tern. Each spring we feel the call.

*   *   *

Anyway, it was early March when the flock with which this bird was flying wheeled away from the ice across the southern storm-swept Pacific, and flying low above the waves they cruised steadily at about twenty miles an hour as their rhythmic beating wings carried them north.

A week later they were feeding along the western coast of Tierra Del Fuego and southern Chile among the off-shore islands with millions of sea birds who make the islands their home.

The terns paused briefly to fill their craws with the abundant marine life in the estuaries. With ten thousand miles ahead of them, their migration was steadily north. Yes, steadily north they flew for nearly eight weeks. They flew west of the snow-capped Andes across the Equator and the Gulf of Panama and on to the Gulf of California, then along the Pacific Coast they flew north to British Columbia.

On and on they went to where Itigak and his flock turned up the Yukon River, still flying north, beyond the Arctic Circle to Koviashuvik.

Now he was here.

Here was where he had been hatched and fed during the endless days of sunshine the year before. Here he would find a mate and continue the cycle of life which carried him from one end of the earth to the other.

*   *   *

As I watched the graceful bird swoop down to the surface of the water to scoop up larvae of the first mosquito hatch, I had made the fantastic journey with him. In my imagination I had made the journey, and now shared his obvious delight in being home. There is no delight that equals coming home.

*   *   *

There were other terns coursing along the lake shore, each stopping to hover with arched body, displaying a wide-spread forked tail before diving into shallows and rising from the cold water with a small fish.

However, it was Itigak, swooping in playful flight, whom I identified from the other arctic terns. I knew him because one foot would not tuck up into his feathers in flight. The red flash of his protruding foot identified him from all the others, and this is how he got the name, Itigak, or foot. In Eskimo, itigak means foot.

*   *   *

How Itigak had been injured was unknown to me. I had wondered about it when I first became aware of him as an immature bird in late summer the year before. Some bird of prey may have attempted to make a meal of him when he was a fledgling, perhaps a jaeger or hawk, attempting to eat him before the predator was driven off by his parents.

Anyway, I thought it more likely that a fish had been the cause. This was because the injury was to a foot. I thought the injury might have been caused by a great northern pike when the young bird wandered too far into the shore grass before it was able to fly.

Whatever happened, it was obviously not disabling. No, it was not disabling, but it did identify him. Yes, it singled him out and gave him value. To me he had value because he was an individual.

I could identify with him.

*   *   *

After the ice melted from the lake, by the second week in June, the terns rested in the sun on a sand spit.

From this point of land, reaching into the lake, they would periodically rise into the air over the water and perform intricate aerial acrobatics. As I watched, they would fly at each other and just when two seemed to be meeting head-on, they would bank aside at the last moment. Then, with a following swoop, they would drop down to the water.

I watched one tern touch the glassy surface with the tip of a vermillion beak, just a touch with its crimson bill, then shoot up into the sky to hover a moment before dropping to catch itself with outstretched wings on a cushion of air.

It was Itigak. The red spot of his foot against his white underside marked him from the other terns.

*   *   *

As I watched Itigak in flight, I became aware that his flying ability was exceptional, even among arctic terns it was exceptional. Or did it just seem exceptional because I could single him out and knew him from the year before? I don't think so.

Anyway, when he dived to scoop up an insect from the mirrored surface, I noted the way he turned to rise with a single sweep of his wings, carrying him several feet above the water before the second stroke of his gull-like wings began their seemingly lazy beat which carried him high above the lake.

The other terns took two strokes on their initial rise but Itigak took only one. He banked more steeply, giving a sense of assurance that he was master of his environment. In the air he was master.

In my mind there was no doubt that Itigak was an exceptional bird among exceptional birds.

*   *   *

During the following week I visited the roosting site on the sand spit periodically, to observe the terns and watch them bow to each other as they returned from fishing or play or bathing.

Their bathing was a ritual. It was a rite that took place in one particular spot in the shallow water near a sandy point. No other place seemed acceptable and each bird bathed in the same area of a few square feet. In an area of a few square feet, a tern would drop to the water, then duck its head and beat its wings in a flurry before flying to the sand spit where it would bow and be bowed to by other terns before settling in the sun.

The birds would bow to each other like Zen monks. When they came out of the water, they would bow. Whenever they returned to the spit, they would bow and then bow again.

*   *   *

Watching a bird take its turn at the bathing spot, I sensed a different quality in the way it splashed and rose from the water. When it landed on the spit its bow to the bird nearest was different from the rest. It was a double bow, quicker and more assertive than the others, and later when it rose to fly out over the lake, my surmise was confirmed when I saw its foot.

I was beginning to recognize Itigak as a distinct personality.

*   *   *

As yet, I was unable to distinguish male from female. While in a flock, I could not tell males from females. Until they began to nest, I knew it would be impossible to guess their sex.

It was easy to see which birds were mates from years before. They paired themselves on the sand spit but I could not tell which was male or female.

Itigak appeared single but whether a she or a he was still unknown to me. It was unknown until late June when I was across the lake gathering firewood.

*   *   *

I had been cutting dead wood and was resting on a projection of land extending into the lake where breezes kept the mosquitos thinned.

Sitting near the edge of the water, I watched two terns flying along the shore calling to each other. With their distinctive cry, they were calling to each other when one of them spotted something in the shallows and hovered, then dropped with a splash and arose six feet above the surface and dove again. This time it arose with a sculpin in its beak. It rose on translucent wings with the tiny fish and joined its companion.

It was Itigak, and he passed the small fish to the tern flying with him.

Itigak had found a mate, and his mate swooped down with the small sculpin to the glassy surface of the water before soaring back into the sky. Itigak followed calling over and over again to her. She made a sharp bank and tossed the fish back to him and he passed it back to her in mid-air and she swallowed it.

I watched them fly along the shore where they repeated the exchange with another tid-bit. They were unaware of me. Wrapped in their relationship they were oblivious of me.

*   *   *

They were not oblivious of me several weeks later when I rowed over to Caribou Island to photograph a loon's nest.

They came flying out to meet me as I approached the shore. The terns came flying out to meet me with high screeching cries and circled over me as I continued to the place I had chosen to land.

Diving at me with red bill open, the birds missed my head by inches as they swooped at me, screeching. They made it very clear that I was not wanted.

When a bird struck the back of my head with its beak, I accepted the message and rowed out into the lake to pick another landing site.

It was Itigak who struck me and he meant business,

which is a peculiar metaphor for an attack by an arctic
tern, but there was no question as to his intent. There
was no question about that.

*   *   *

I was used to terns diving at me. I had approached
their nesting sites in order to photograph the dull green
eggs with their black mottling which so blended into the
rocks, sand and grass that they were practically invisible.
I was used to their cries and swooping passes, but this
furor of Itigak was something else.

I decided to treat him with particular respect since
I had seen him plummet unerringly for small fish. I was
aware that he could strike an eye with the same accuracy.

Anyway, I had become so involved with the life of this
exceptional creature that I felt a responsibility for the
welfare of those two eggs which he and his mate had
flown so far to produce.

Besides, we were neighbors. We were residents of the
same community in which they respected our rights and
territory. We would respect theirs.

*   *   *

Now that I knew where Itigak and his mate had settled,
I planned to keep an eye on them and their nest because
the tern's eggs were vulnerable to many predators.

Exposed on the beach, in what could hardly be called
a nest, the eggs were vulnerable in a shallow depression
scooped out of sand and gravel. When the parents are
away, the camouflage of the mottled eggs is their only
protection. When one of the parents is gathering food
it is difficult for a single bird to defend the nest from
more than one predator. It is a difficult task.

*   *   *

This is the way it was a few days later when I visited
the island and Itigak's mate was being harassed by two
parasitic jaegers. When she flew screeching at one jaeger,

the other would swoop toward her eggs in the slight depression on the shore. This forced her to abandon her chase to drive off the other falcon-like intruder.

As I rowed closer to shore with the aim of being helpful, she turned her attention to me. I was just another predator after her eggs as far as she was concerned, and I quickly realized my presence would make it possible for a jaeger to take an egg while she was flying at me. I pulled out into the lake.

Rowing out from shore, I heard the shrill call of another tern streaking across the water toward me.

Itigak, who had been hunting along the shore, apparently heard the cries of his mate and he dipped at me as he rushed toward the jaeger. Diving toward the nest, Itigak's fury was sensed by the jaegers because the bird at which he darted with fierce shrieks and gaping beak flew off across the lake toward the far shore. The other quickly followed.

*　　*　　*

While watching this drama, I was not aware that the breeze had caused me to drift closer to the bank and Itigak turned his fury on me. He dived at me while I rowed out of the invisible territorial circle where my presence was unacceptable.

Being helpful usually makes things worse. Nearly always it is anything but helpful to be helpful without being asked. Yes it is.

*　　*　　*

I continued to visit the terns, but kept our agreed-upon distance, while they took turns incubating the precious eggs. They took turns.

When she was on the nest, Itigak would fly in with a gift of insects, or a small fish, before replacing her on the eggs while she sailed out to hunt.

*　　*　　*

Finally it was time for the eggs to hatch. It was time, and I wanted to be present. However, a storm moved in with heavy rain and wind churned the lake into white caps for several days. With the churning from wind and rain, I was confined to the vicinity of our cabin.

*   *   *

After the storm passed, I returned to Caribou Island. The terns were not there to fly at me from their nesting site. They were not there, and it was strangely quiet as I walked the shore examining it carefully.

I could find no sign of the depression where the eggs had been. There was no sign that there had ever been a nest. The heavy rain had beaten down the sand and every few feet gullies had washed the pebbles to the lake edge. A gully had probably formed where the terns had nested.

*   *   *

Rowing around the island on my return, I heard a familiar disturbed cry as a white form came winging toward me making a low pass overhead with open beak.

Was another pair of terns nesting on this side of the island unknown to me? Was there a different pair I wondered when another bird dived at me screeching its displeasure?

I recognized the red foot.

Then Itigak's mate again joined in the attack, swooping at me before turning to fly over the beach. There, below her, I saw them. Yes, I saw two fluffy yellow chicks awkwardly waddling along the sandy shore.

*   *   *

Pulling out of range of the parents' attacks, I watched them for hours. They never left the chicks alone. Always, one parent remained close, talking in a soft call, while the other flew across the lake for food.

When the hunting parent returned, mouths opened

wide as the adult thrust its beak into the open maws to disgorge the meal.

While Itigak was feeding the chicks, his mate's strong wings carried her out of sight across the water to return in fifteen or twenty minutes with her contribution.

Except for their interest in being fed, when a parent returned with food, the two downy chicks seemed primarily interested in exploration of the shoreline. In their exploration, they already had traveled nearly half a mile from where they were hatched. This was dangerous because they were most vulnerable to predators now. They were most vulnerable because they were unable to fly. However, their mottled-yellow color was an excellent camouflage. In the shore sedges they were impossible to see when not in motion.

*   *   *

Hanging my camera around my neck, I tied the boat to the island shore. I tied the boat a few hundred feet away and approached the baby terns through a thick grove of dark spruce trees. I crept inland through the trees, which would protect me from Itigak's attack, so I could get a photograph of the chicks.

I wanted to photograph the chicks but with my appearance at the edge of the trees, and with the excited cries and dives at me by the parents, the chicks panicked. One scrambled into the undergrowth on the bank and the other waded through the reeds at shoreline and swam out into the water.

As the chick swam along the edge of the sedges, I saw a stir on the surface. A swirl began about twenty feet away and I knew immediately what it was but felt helpless as the swirl became a swift-moving wedge aimed straight for the chick. The great northern pike never deviated as the moving surface marked his course like a torpedo. Like a torpedo, the wedge moved straight toward the chick. There was a roiling of water and splash of tail fin as it broke the surface. Then a flash of silver glinted as the great northern pike turned back into deeper water.

The chick was gone.

*   *   *

It happened so swiftly that it was several seconds before I could assimilate what had taken place. I moved back into the trees and returned to the boat. I returned to the boat from where I could see Itigak's mate on the shore with the other chick. She was on shore with the other chick while Itigak circled above them before flying off to gather food as if nothing had happened.

*   *   *

And there I sat.

I felt numb, but more than that I felt responsible. I was responsible for the loss of the chick.

Itigak and his mate seemed unaware of the loss. I felt terrible. I was not even trying to be helpful, which would have been bad enough, but in my wish to be an observer I became part of the tragedy. In my ignorance, I was responsible like we are all responsible in our ignorance.

Our excuse is ignorance. Always, our excuse is ignorance. But we are still responsible.

*   *   *

For a long time I sat watching the terns move along the shore. The parents fed their single chick and each in turn soared off to forage for food. My thoughts were fixed on the ways of terns and pike and people. Of the three, only the human being is introspective, seeks meaning and tries to discover a larger purpose.

In my introspective mood, I watched Itigak stop in mid-air above the shallows to hover on beating wings, then plunge into the water to rise with a small fish in his beak. I wondered how I would feel if I knew as much about that small fish as I did about Itigak? The fish was probably a freshwater sculpin which basks in the sandy shallows of the lake. It is found in eastern Siberia as well as western Alaska. It once occupied the Bering land bridge when people first immigrated to the new world.

Today it was food for Itigak's chick.

*   *   *

Moving stiffly from where I had been sitting so long on the wooden seat of the boat, I opened the fishing box and selected a large plug with three sets of sharp triple hooks. I fastened it to the steel leader of my casting rod. There was a particular great northern pike I felt I had to catch for our supper if it took me the rest of the day.

*   *   *

As for Itigak, I last saw him turn against the blue of the sky when the alders were red from early frosts. His mate and offspring turned with him. Days were swiftly growing shorter and the arctic terns are birds of light. The sun of Tierra Del Fuego calls and the terns of Koviashuvik have a long journey ahead.

So do we.

*For all men strive to grasp what
they do not know, while none
strive to grasp what they already
know; and all strive to discredit
what they do not excel in, while
none strive to discredit what they
do excel in. This is why there is
chaos.*

CHUANG TZU, 369-286 B.C.

11
Voice from the Wilderness
On the trans-Alaska pipeline project

I went to work for the trans-Alaska pipeline project when
they were building the trans-Alaska pipeline. I went to
work as a counselor in camps north of the Yukon River.
So did Billie.

In camps we served, north of the Yukon, we were
called Site-Counselors.

* * *

Before I went to work on the pipeline and before the
project was approved by Congress, I spoke at the Department of the Interior Environmental Impact Hearings in
Anchorage, Alaska.

This is what I said:

"My name is Sam Wright. I am a resident of the Brooks
Range, approximately eighty miles northeast of Bettles
Field, north of the Arctic Circle. I am not here to testify

against the development of Alaska's oil resources, but rather to speak for her greatest resource, wilderness.

"One definition of wilderness is that very few people inhabit it. Therefore, there are few voices to speak from within. As a resident in the Brooks Range, I feel it not only my privilege, but my duty to speak for those voiceless who might never be heard if I do not choose to represent them.

"Who are these voiceless?

"They are those who share this planet-spaceship with us; whose presence here defines our human qualities and concerns as much as any social, human institution. They are the caribou who have called this their home for thousands of years. They are the wolf, the lynx, the fox, the wolverine. They are the majestic Dall sheep, the grizzly bear, the gyrfalcon and the arctic loon. They are the millions of shore birds and the arctic tern, who yearly flies eleven thousand miles from Antarctica to nest by the lakes of this wilderness.

"Who will speak for those spruce trees which struggle up the Dietrich River, moving timber line north . . . trees whose diameter is seldom more than eight inches, but were seedlings when George Washington was inaugurated our first President? Who will speak for solitude . . . one of the last places where the ancient sounds of life can be heard without the whine of gears or the drone of engines? Who will speak for those of our own species to come, those who will have no place left in the world uncontaminated by their predecessor's self-righteous need to convert everything, including beauty and solitude, into dollars? Who will speak for this last great wilderness to remain wilderness? For if it goes, it will never be returned. I have no choice. I must speak because I am not voiceless, and this is my home.

"My wife and I are residents of the Brooks Range in northern Alaska. We live within ten miles of the proposed trans-Alaska pipeline corridor route along the Koyokuk and Dietrich rivers. We know first-hand the wildlife, the long dark winters and the endless summer sun north of the Arctic Circle.

"We have chosen to live in this last great wilderness, disturbing it as little as possible and becoming a part of its ecology. One reason for this choice several years ago was the recognition that at this moment in history this great wilderness is doomed unless voices speak out in its behalf. And certainly a voice should come from the wilderness itself.

"For myself and those other inhabitants who with humans share this last undefiled place on this continent, those whom I represent in this appeal, I say that all the oil in Alaska is not worth the loss of this last great wilderness.

"This wilderness is the heritage of us all. And since it is the heritage of us all, we should all have a voice in the decisions which will determine its fate.

"However, the destruction of our heritage has already begun without our being heard — without a permit from the Interior Department for the pipeline and the haul road that would run beside it. Caravans of trailers and heavy equipment have already been hauled up the Dietrich River into the wilderness of the Brooks Range. Bulldozers have already cut a swath north of timber line. For months, great Hercules aircraft flew regularly over our small isolated cabin in the wilderness, to Galbraith Lake, on the north slope of the range, hauling in equipment for construction of the oil pipeline and haul road over the pass. Helicopter loads of survey and construction crews, with their attendant debris, were flown into the few lakes in our area to fish for trout, which, in the northern cold, take ten to twenty years to reach maturity.

"If the bulldozing, construction camps, airfields and traffic can function without a Department of the Interior pipeline permit, there is no question that to grant one will mark the end of our last great wilderness.

"If we permit the construction of a pipeline and its accompanying haul road to be built through this wilderness, we will not have moved forward or confronted the future with vitality and courage. We will, instead, have taken a giant step backward. For real progress is to recognize, preserve and wisely use our resources. And our greatest resource in the greatest jeopardy, because it can never be replaced or recreated, is wilderness.

"We cannot plead ignorance today as we have in the past. If we permit the domestication and ultimate destruction of this wilderness, we shall be condemned by our posterity for having deprived them of their heritage.

"Our choice is not between wilderness and oil. Our struggle is not between oil companies and the public. Our common responsibility, in the light of overwhelming scientific and technical evidence presented by those who do not have a vested economic interest in the decision confronting us, is to save the wilderness.

"I cannot speak for other people. They have a voice of their own. But for myself and my voiceless neighbors in the wilderness of the Brooks Range, I appeal not only to the Secretary of the Interior, the President of the United States, my fellow Americans and Alaskans, but also and particularly to the representatives of the seven oil companies who formed the Alyeska Pipeline Service Corporation, to save this last great wilderness. When it goes, there is no other."

*   *   *

Five years later Billie and I were working for the seven oil companies.

It was not called Seven Oil Companies. We were employed by the Alyeska Pipeline Service Company, formed by the seven oil companies, to construct the trans-Alaska oil pipeline.

We went to work for the Alyeska Pipeline Service Company as counselors because we were asked. We wanted the pipeline finished as quickly and efficiently as possible. Yes, we wanted the pipeline project completed and contractors out of the wilderness as soon as possible. And, there was also the money. Yes, the money.

We needed the money, but mostly we needed the pipeline finished. It could not be stopped, after Congress voted for it, but it could be finished. For money, we helped finish the pipeline project. For money, we were counselors in construction camps north of the Yukon.

*   *   *

Not only for money.

It was an adventure. We are explorers and there had never been counselors before like we were to be counselors, and no one had explored what it was to be a counselor in a trans-Alaska pipeline project camp.

Anyway, I went to work two months before Billie and it began with a physical examination and orientation process with twenty-three males and one female. It began one day at Fort Wainwright outside Fairbanks with the filling in of forms.

Posted on a wall in the orientation room was a large sign for spelling the words penicillin, Dietrich, Isabel Pass, Livengood, Prudhoe Bay, tonsillectomy, Fluor, appendectomy. These must have been the most misspelled, but more important were directions for following the painted stripes on the concrete floor.

Red line, I.D.; yellow line, Arctic clothing; white line,

Rest Room. Everywhere today there are painted lines to follow. Even if they don't show, we follow the stripes someone has painted for us.

*   *   *

By eight o'clock that evening I was on an airplane looking down at the white ridges, peaks and canyons of the Brooks Range in bright moonlight. In the moonlight, in the middle of March, we crossed the Brooks Range and flew across the barren white tundra of the north slope to Happy Valley. In ice fog we landed at the pipeline camp of Happy Valley where I was to be On Site-Counselor for Eskimos, Indians, and Aleuts, as well as the non-native construction workers and engineers.

*   *   *

The next morning I was awakened by a voice on the public address system. In a rich baritone it said, "Good morning, it is seven o'clock. The temperature is thirty-seven degrees below zero." It said, "The wind is five knots from the south with a chill factor of forty-five degrees below zero and there is ice fog in camp. Have a nice day."

That is what the voice said, so in the spirit of adventure I went down the hall of the trailer-barracks to the wash room.

*   *   *

The camp of Happy Valley was really two camps, A and B. They were called A camp on one side of the trans-Alaska pipeline haul road and B Camp on the other side of the road. Like towns in America that were divided by the railroad, some people lived on the other side of the tracks.

Happy Valley B Camp was the other side of the tracks. The place to be was among the engineers and staff in A Camp. My headquarters were in A Camp. In a temporary camp of six hundred people it was interesting that we were already divided into we and they. Or, A and B.

One of the premises we have held since the early Greeks is that everything is divided into either/or. Yes, divided into A or B. Even in camps which were not divided by the haul road there was always the premise of we and they.

Anyhow, I saw my role as a counselor to narrow the gap between we and they. The obvious problems with which we were concerned could nearly always be seen as those of we and they. As a counselor it was we and they that dominated the construction workers' lives but I wonder if this is reality. Maybe our premise is wrong. I wonder.

*   *   *

Well, Happy Valley was an adventure. And north of Happy Valley there was a camp called Franklin Bluffs where I was also the counselor. This was also an adventure where eight hundred people lived on the white, windy flats less than forty miles from the Arctic Ocean.

We had a sign at Franklin Bluffs to locate us north south east and west. It said: North Pole 500 miles, Fairbanks Alaska 500 miles, Toktoyaktuk Canada 500 miles, Siberia USSR 500 miles.

And there we were.

Yes, there we were making money and bringing crude oil through Alaska so people could fly to exotic places like the Australian outback and the Eskimo village at Toktoyaktuk.

But mostly we were making money, which was really why eight hundred people were living on the arctic flats.

*   *   *

And so I was a counselor at the camp at Franklin Bluffs and at Happy Valley A and B, and at Chandalar and Dietrich camps. And Billie was counselor at Coldfoot and Prospect camps north of the Yukon.

We said we would only serve camps north of the Yukon River because we lived north of the Yukon at Koviashuvik which was not far from Dietrich camp by helicopter. It was not far by helicopter, but in values like self-reliance, solitude, joy and freedom it was a million miles. A million miles.

* * *

Values are what I am most interested in, why we have the values we have and how we change them and why they are valuable and if they really are valuable. Mostly if they really are.

Freedom is an interesting value. Freedom from fear, anxiety, hate and hostility is a novel concept for most of humankind. Yes it is. We can no more imagine what a society without these impediments to self-realization would be like than Neanderthal Man could have imagined the technological revolution.

In the pipeline camps people were free from concerns for food, shelter and health care. These were there for everyone. Everyone had clean towels and housekeeping with beds made, and everybody was making money.

Everyone was making more money than ever before. Someone had written on the wall of a barracks hallway at Franklin Bluffs camp:

NEVER

IN THE ANNALS

OF CONSTRUCTION HISTORY

HAVE SO MANY

DONE SO LITTLE

FOR SO MUCH

But people did not feel free. They were anxious and afraid. They were not free of hate and hostility. They saw the environment as hostile and they hated the cold.

Yes, they hated the cold and they were anxious about the future and were afraid of their employers and as counselors we learned that everything was we and they. Freedom is more than security.

*   *   *

At Koviashuvik we learned that freedom is responsibility. At Koviashuvik we are free but not of responsibility. At Koviashuvik we are responsible because we are free. Freedom and responsibility are not A and B at Koviashuvik. They are the same thing.

*   *   *

In the pipeline camps people were not free. They were not responsible. They had security but did not feel responsible like most of us do not feel responsible for actions of large institutions and governments.

Where we are not responsible we are not free like the Russians are not free because they do not have responsibility. They have security but not freedom. This is why we have carved on the purlin of our cabin at Koviashuvik:

SECURE US FROM SECURITY NOW AND FOREVER. AMEN.

*   *   *

We had lots of adventures in the pipeline camps. From counseling seven official minorities to arbitrating labor problems and dealing with murder.

When we talk informally about our adventures on the pipeline project people say why don't you write a book?

I tried to write a book about the trans-Alaska pipeline project but it did not say what I wanted it to say. It never said what I wanted it to say because I never identified with the project. In the same way I never identified with the Office of Scientific Research and Development where I was involved in secret weapons development in World War II. That was another book I didn't write.

In the world of communication, what you don't say or do can be as much a statement as what is said or done. The letter you did not write can get an astounding reply. The form you did not fill in can produce an amazing response, particularly from the Internal Revenue Service.

*   *   *

Well, Billie and I were Site-Counselors on the trans-Alaska pipeline project until there was a reduction in force as the project neared completion.

We were helicopterd back to Koviashuvik but it was not the same because we were not the same. Koviashuvik had not changed, but we had changed and Alaska had changed like the world has changed since we exploded a device near Alamogordo, New Mexico.

The world is not the same. Everything has changed.

*   *   *

Everything will always change. We know that. But how it changes and what the changes will be can no longer be left to the will of Zeus, Odin or Yahweh.

A faith of adventure is returning in new forms to be explored. It is about time.

*We are a culture in transition look-
ing for a new way of being in the
world that affirms us as persons and
manifests harmony with our planet.*

DAVID SPANGLER

12

Transformation

The domestication of everything

After ten winters north of the Arctic Circle in Alaska,
we decided to spend a winter in the lower forty-eight.
People in the other states do not think of themselves
as lower but they are if the North Pole is the top of the
world.

An astronomer told me it was not the top. He said
astronomers view the South Pole as the top of the world.

However, I know the South Pole is not the top because
Santa Claus lives at the top of the world. He lives at the
North Pole. Ask anyone. Even people who do not believe
in Santa Claus know where he lives.

*   *   *

Anyway, we decided to spend a winter in the lower
forty-eight. We were not far into the lower forty-eight
because we spent the winter just south of Canada on
the border of Washington and Idaho, along the Pend
Oreille River. We spent the winter in an old ranch house

which was too big for the stove. I was once told I was too big for my britches, not that the britches were too small. I wasn't really too big for my britches but the house was too big for the stove.

*   *   *

We liked the mountains and the forests of Douglas fir and the giant arborvitae and larch along the Pend Oreille River. Larch is called tamarack and giant arborvitae trees are called red cedar on the Pend Oreille. Along the Pend Oreille, people will argue that arborvitae are cedars and larch are tamarack, like a char is a trout and a reindeer a caribou in Alaska.

*   *   *

Yes, the house was too big for the stove and we were cold all winter. We were cold and shivered. Even when we were warm we shivered because the snow was wet and the air was wet and it thawed between snowstorms. We were cold. Even when we were warm we felt cold.

We liked the beauty in the country of the Pend Oreille but not the winter. North of the Arctic Circle we like winter where it is warm when it is cold. We are warm at Koviashuvik when the thermometer registers cold but along the Pend Oreille we were cold.

*   *   *

We then spent a winter in the mountains of central Arizona.

*   *   *

I had worked with a survey crew in the Sierra Ancha mountains of central Arizona the year I graduated from high school. The Sierra Ancha mountains had never been fully surveyed. They had been declared unsurveyable before 1900. By 1938 no land was considered unsurveyable. In 1938 the United States General Land Office was surveying the Sierra Ancha mountains and I was there.

*   *   *

On mules and horses, we packed our food and equipment into the rugged mountains. Through manzanita, catclaw and mountain mahogany, we climbed into the yellow pines beneath Aztec Peak. There we set up camp.

From the central camp, our three-man survey crews went out each day to measure the land and mark Township and Section Corners. We set corners so maps in Washington D.C. would indicate where everything was. People want to know where everything is. Even where there isn't anything, people want a map to show where it is.

*　　*　　*

I had not been back to the Sierra Ancha montains in forty years. Now that I was back nothing seemed changed beneath Aztec Peak. Nothing had really changed except trees had grown taller and the area we surveyed is now called the Sierra Ancha Wilderness. No new roads are allowed.

Even though we measured Townships, and put them on the map, there is no town in the wilderness. There will be no town unless Congress changes the law.

I hope not.

*　　*　　*

Billie and I spent a winter in the Sierra Ancha. Then we built a house of rocks. Like an Indian pueblo, we built a rock cabin on a hill overlooking Buzzard Roost Mesa. In the Sierra Ancha we built a dwelling but we went back to Koviashuvik before freeze-up.

We always go back to Koviashuvik. North of the Arctic Circle is our home. Wherever we live, Koviashuvik is home.

*　　*　　*

At Koviashuvik, the first snow of autumn arrived quietly in the night and transformed Mount Truth with a dusting of white while the bronze willows and crimson alders shouted a cacophony of color among golden birches.

The world was transformed. It was transformed across the lake and where I stood. I stood in front of our log cabin in a world that was transformed. So was I.

This is what I want to tell about. Transformation.

*   *   *

Actually, transformation cannot be written about.

Transformation takes place and there it is. As Shunryu Suzuki said, this particular expression of it is not it and yet at the same time it is it.

For a while this is it, for the smallest particle of time this is it. But it is not always so. No, the very next instant it is not so.

*   *   *

Well anyway, Billie and I flew the two hundred miles north from Fairbanks with our friend, Syd, in his small amphibian. We flew north, after being weathered in at Fairbanks for several days, which gave us time to shop for supplies and spend an afternoon at the Alaska State Fair.

It was an afternoon of laughing children and barnyard smells, with cotton candy and red, yellow, blue and silver balloons escaping into a turquoise sky to drift against the northern spruce-green hills. It was hard to accept the weather report of a front moving in between us and our destination, two hundred miles north.

*   *   *

"Hello, Sam. Are you in town for supplies?" a voice said.

I saw a familiar face behind the wire of an animal pen. The face was familiar but I did not recognize the man with his wife and two small children. Who is he, I wondered? Where have I known him before? What is his name? The wife and children are not familiar. Then he smiled. In the transformation I recognized him.

In the transformation of a smile I recognized Clint, whom I knew as a radio dispatcher in a northern camp of the trans-Alaska pipeline project. I remembered the enthusiasm with which he promoted Billie's book among the construction workers. Now he has been transformed. Yes, he has been transformed. He said he was now working on the north slope of the Brooks Range for an oil company and has a family in Fairbanks. He plans to build a home on the outskirts of town.

*　　*　　*

Transformation.

As I stood in front of our cabin, Truth was transformed.

Our meals of northern pike and lake trout have been transformed into a contentment of body and soul almost forgotten during the past months of busyness in the world of telephones, freeways and social responsibilities.

This morning's radio report of conflicts in the Near East, with congressional and presidential maneuvering and inference of economic doom, have all been transformed into minor bits and pieces of a world that also contains millions of years of living with seasons, stars and migrations. Yes, a million years of laughter, death and birth.

Even so, in the ignorance of our stupidity we could end it all—transform it all forever. Yes, forever, which is one hell of a long time.

This is why I feel compelled to write about transformation. It can go two ways. Like everything in the world, it can go either way.

*　　*　　*

Words are used to transform reality and sometimes we believe it happens. We believe the words and not the reality. Such as missiles called peace-makers and atomic weapons called defense.

*   *   *

When I take our winter meat, I actually kill a caribou or moose. Yes, I kill a moose and butcher it. I transform it into winter meat.

With words we transform killing into taking, and butchering into preparing. We take our winter meat without reference to specific game, such as caribou or Dall sheep. Even the word, game, transforms the act. I do not see our activity as sport. It is not a game. Sport implies an element of play. Hunting for us is not sport.

Even the word, hunting, which once had worthy antecedents and still has positive values, has been transformed into fair-chase. Costumed people on horses, following a pack of dogs, after a terrified fox released from a cage is called hunting. There is no fair-chase today. Even in Alaska, where I am a hunter, there is no fair-chase; although there are still positive values in the hunting syndrome, it is not fair-chase.

I hunt, kill and butcher our caribou or moose with a quality of excitement and awe because this is the way we lived for millions of years. Physically and psychologically and socially I am a hunter. We are all hunters, even though we have transformed hunting into a sport. Transformed it into games like football, business and war.

At Koviashuvik we have transformed football into wood cutting, and business into food gathering and hunting. We would transform war if we could. Yes we would.

*   *   *

As I said, this is about transformation, which can go either way. So we went back to Arizona for the winter. We settled in Pleasant Valley. We wintered beneath the Mogollon Rim in the Sierra Ancha mountains.

Every year we return to Koviashuvik, like the birds return to Koviashuvik, because it is home.

We are also at home in the Sierra Ancha, where we visit in the winter like the arctic terns visit Tierra Del Fuego but nest at Koviashuvik.

Our nest is at Koviashuvik.

*   *   *

In Pleasant Valley our life is different from Koviashuvik.

Even though we live near a wilderness in Arizona we have a telephone and can see television, and Billie was President of the Library Board and I was President of the Pleasant Valley Community Medical Center.

There are not many people in Pleasant Valley but they try to do everything people do in a city.

*   *   *

Now we live in two places, and it has transformed us.

Even though we are the same people, we are different in Arizona because the environment is different. We are different in Alaska because we wintered in Arizona. We like being different because it is difference that makes us what we are.

Difference is an interesting concept if you think about it, which we don't very often. It is not an event or a thing. When difference occurs across time, we call it change or transformation.

*   *   *

Well, as I said, there are positive values in the hunting syndrome and one of them is that it gets the sportsman out of suburbia and into an environment we call nature. Even though suburbia is as much nature as the countryside, it is different.

The nature of animals in a zoo is different from those in the wild, so we speak of the nature of animals in a crowded cage as different from the nature of animals in their natural habitat.

What is our natural habitat?

A biological historian would say that in a natural habitat the life style of the human species is gatherer and hunter. Only recently did we shift into the domestication of plants and animals and ourselves. Ourselves, which we call civilization. We call it civilization and give it a high value in contrast to what we call the uncivilized life of our pre-domesticated ways.

*   *   *

But listen to this.

We are beginning to question civilization. Today we see our systems of domestication binding us more and more into strictures as tight as the stanchions that hold the domesticated dairy cow for milk and artificial insemination.

With civilized atomic deterrents, I do not feel a bit safer. And the models of civilized behaviorist psychologists scare the shit out of me. (This more a literalism than a metaphor.)

*   *   *

There is no blueprint for the future, but there is something very important in the quality of our lives at Koviashuvik that needs to be recaptured.

I am not recommending a return to the natural world of our forebears because it is not physically possible. Besides, the world of our forebears no longer exists. However, something important is at stake. We know with knowledge as deep as the marrow of our bones that something important is at stake as we make the transition from what we are to what we can become.

*   *   *

Before we talk about becoming, we had better know what we are. We know we are more than the machines and systems we create and try to imitate. Yes, in a dim, unrecognized way this may be why millions load their cars and motorhomes, at considerable sacrifice to comfort, and head for crowded campgrounds each summer.

*   *   *

Anyway, Billie and I prefer moose to domestic beef, and a cabin in the wilderness to a split-level tract house near a university campus. We are probably throwbacks and need to restructure our priorities.

Sometimes, in Pleasant Valley, we wonder about our priorities but never at Koviashuvik. Never.

If a person shows that such things as wood, stones and the like, being many are also one, we admit he shows the coexistence of the one and the many, but he does not show that the many are one or the one many; he is uttering not a paradox but a truism.

PLATO, 428-348 B.C.

13
On They Went
A visit to the bristlecones

Since we now dwell in Arizona, as well as Alaska, people ask us where we live and we cannot answer their question the way they want it answered. This is because they say we cannot live in two places at the same time. You live either here or there, they say. You live in one place or another.

We live in Koviashuvik.

No matter where we dwell we live in Koviashuvik. Even in our old Volkswagen camper, on our way to visit the oldest living things in the Inyo Mountains of California, we live in Koviashuvik.

Even on our way we are at home.

*   *   *

We were on our way to visit the bristlecone pines.

The oldest living things known are bristlecone pines growing between eleven and twelve thousand feet above sea level in the Inyo Mountains. There are trees living there now which were growing in the same spot when the great Egyptian pyramids were being built. Yes, when Moses received the Ten Commandments, these living trees were many years old. They were old when Socrates questioned youth in the streets of Athens and they had been growing for more than two thousand years before Jesus walked the Galilean shore.

Today they are still alive and they are old.

*   *   *

Anyway, we went to visit these ancient pines because I had been among them years before when Edmund Schulman first discovered a tree over four thousand years old in the nineteen-fifties. I was excited when I heard about it and visited the Inyo Mountains where I took borings of the ancient bristlecone pines with a Swedish increment borer. With a Swedish increment borer, I made holes in ancient trees to determine their age.

It is interesting that increment boring instruments were Swedish when I was determining the age of trees. There may have been American increment borers made in Japan or Taiwan but they were always called Swedish, like cheese is called Swiss. When cheese is holey it is called Swiss.

When trees are holy they are called sacred. They are sacred because there is hidden meaning in them. I discovered hidden meaning in a living tree that was a growing seedling before Zeus, Yahweh, Odin, God, Allah or The Christ were invented. Yes, living before they were invented.

*   *   *

After many years Billie and I returned to the ancient bristlecone forest, because we had seen a section I had cut from a four-thousand-year-old bristlecone tree and given to the Alice Eastwood Museum of the California Academy of Sciences in San Francisco. In the museum it did not seem real even though I had cut it. Behind glass it did not seem real so we went to where the trees were real.

We drove to the Ancient Bristlecone Pine Forest where trees were living and real after four thousand years. After four thousand years still living and real.

It was not easy to get there.

It is never easy to get where things are real but it is always worth the effort.

*   *   *

It was not easy to get there because we had to go by way of Phoenix. It was one hundred and twelve degrees in Phoenix where Billie and I had made a speaking commitment, so we left from Phoenix at four-thirty the next morning because we had miles of desert to cross. In July it is cooler in the morning if you are crossing the desert without an air-conditioner.

We left Phoenix through Sun City. You have to be old to live in Sun City. Early in the morning we drove through Sun City where the suppressed roar of thousands of air-conditioners could be heard. Only air-conditioners could be heard in the early morning in Sun City where you have to be old. You have to be old but not necessarily wise, only old and have money, but mostly old.

Bristlecone pines are old. Where we were going they are thousands of years old, but there are also young ones. Unlike Sun City, there are always young ones.

*   *   *

Then we watched the sun rise along the Hassayampa River. The doves were cooing along the Hassayampa as we drove into Wickenburg. We drove along the Hassayampa and into Wickenburg for breakfast.

*   *   *

As I said, it wasn't easy. The car would not start because the solenoid on the starter was stuck and I had to crawl under the camper on the scorching pavement. In the old mining town of Wickenburg, I had to reach up by the hot engine on the sweltering pavement. I reached up by the hot engine and burned my arm. But a mockingbird sang from the power line and we had a thermos of hot coffee and were soon on our way to Kingman and Boulder Dam on the Colorado River where water was running over the spillways for the first time.

Water was pouring over the spillways from Lake Mead and we were there to see it. It was real.

*   *   *

Then we drove into Las Vegas, Nevada.

Down the Las Vegas Strip, along the unbelievable casinos of the Las Vegas Strip, in the middle of the day we drove down the Strip to where we had to turn at the famous Caesar's Palace casino which blocked the street. It blocked the street and we had to turn at the Palace, which we had seen on television, beamed by satellite around the world.

Millions know the Palace. Yes, millions of people know about the Palace, but only a few know a bristlecone called Alpha. Alpha was a seedling when the original Strip was called Gomorrah and Las Vegas was just a desert water hole.

*   *   *

Water holes are scarce north of Las Vegas.

Indian Springs was just a water hole in the desert before the Nellis Air Force Range and Nuclear Testing Site made it famous.

Indian Springs is now a nuclear target. It seems strange that it is a nuclear missile target when only a handful of people live at Indian Springs. It is still just a waterhole where we bought gasoline and filled a water bottle. When a low flying Air Force jet roared overhead, it was not strange that it was a target.

Then we drove on to the next ancient water hole which today is called Beatty.

In Nevada every town has a casino, usually a restaurant. In Beatty we ate with slot machines in a cafe called a casino. Beatty is also called the gateway to Death Valley. It is.

*   *   *

As I said, it was July and the desert was a glare when we turned west off the highway north of Death Valley. We turned through the Magruder Mountains up Westgard Pass into the White Mountains of the Inyo National Forest. There, we made a dry camp at nine thousand feet above sea level among piñon pines and junipers. We camped in clear mountain air in the silence of the mountains. In the silence of the mountains we watched the sparks of our campfire glitter toward the stars and we were at home, like the bristlecone pines were at home, here on the mountain above us. We were not really like the pines. They were at home here before our ancestors learned to write.

*   *   *

At sun-up a Clark's Nutcracker called from the top of a juniper. Across Owens Valley the Sierra Nevada Mountains stood like a wall with its twelve thousand foot jagged crest catching the sunshine. While we sipped our coffee over the sweet smelling smoke from our breakfast fire, the snowy crest formed a line of rosy peaks against the deep blue.

Then we drove on up the mountain between ten and eleven thousand feet and there we were among the bristlecone pines.

*   *   *

There we were among the world's oldest living things.

I hiked up to Alpha, the first living tree dated older than four thousand years. After four thousand three hundred years, Alpha was mostly a dead snag with twisted branches reaching up in the thin air.

When asked, what is beauty, Gregory Bateson said, seeing the pattern that connects. He said, seeing the pattern that connects, and there it was.

*   *   *

There seems to be no way that our mind or senses can penetrate the mysteries of life and lead to the heart of reality. The human mind and senses seem unable to uncover or report on the inner nature of life and the universe because knowledge gained through sense perception and use of the mind is always partial and limited. The more we know the less we know is a truism. It is a paradox which carries a truth. Yes it does.

Anyway, through the use of our senses and our minds we chop the world up into bits and pieces and label this a mountain and that a tree, which they are. Yes, they really are, but we also know that reality is one and it is somehow false to fragment it.

*   *   *

Well, Billie and I are aware that there is a deeper element in reality than that which we experience on the mere surface, and to make contact with this quality is a need of the human spirit.

It brought us back to these ancient living trees.

Even here, among the bristlecone pines, we do not confuse feeling intensely with knowing certainly. We can feel very intense about an idea which is obviously false.

The truth of an idea or conception is not the intensity of feeling it induces. It is its correspondence with the facts of existence.

What are the facts of existence?

Bristlecone pines for one.

History is not making the sense it once seemed to make, and we seem to be in the position of the eighteenth century when fossils were being discovered but nobody knew what to make of them.

WILLIAM IRWIN THOMPSON

14
Tree Planting
To jump three thousand years

Four small bands of Dall sheep watched us from across the North Fork of the Koyokuk River. They watched Billie and me climb up a thousand feet around the mountain cut. At the top of the Brooks Range, we made our way north of timber line above raw gullies as we struggled along a sheep trail to a level spot to rest.

*   *   *

On a promontory across the gorge a single ram stood overlooking the canyon below. Through my field glasses his horns were a full curl, so important to the trophy hunter.

Billie and I were standing on a similar outjutting across the canyon and I felt that surge of assuredness which wildness gives so freely.

There we stood, where Robert Marshall and his companions may have stood to look across this same canyon years before, and felt this exhilaration.

Little has changed here since then. Little has changed
because the nearest pavement is still nearby three hundred miles away in Fairbanks. The closest settlement is
the small Eskimo village in Anaktuvuk Pass more than
fifty air miles west of us.

*   *   *

Bob Marshall had given the name Barrenland to the
creek where we camped the past three days. The description in his journal could have been this particular summer instead of 1939:

> We stopped for lunch at the edge of the foaming white
> water dropping from a bright green basin entirely devoid
> of any sort of tree growth. While Jesse and Nuterwick
> were making tea, Harvey and I followed that tributary
> upstream a couple of miles to a point where we could
> see the entire head of this valley. It was fascinating in
> its barrenness. So we called the drainage Barrenland
> Creek.

*   *   *

Robert Marshall had a theory that the northern timber
line in this part of Alaska was not the result of unfavor-
able environment for tree growth, but that there had not
been time enough since the last ice sheet receded for
the forest to migrate farther north.

One reason for this view was the fast growth of the
most northerly trees. The spruce trees at northern timber
line had the same growth patterns as those farther south.

*   *   *

Marshall wrote in his journal:

> According to my theory, the spruce stands eventually
> will extend to the Arctic Divide and cross over into the
> sheltered valleys north of the divide. If this is so it should
> be possible simply by sowing seed to extend the timber
> line far north of where it now is.

* * *

If trees were successfully grown in the next valley north of the present timber line, it would be an advancement of time for timber line of about three thousand years. Based on Marshall's estimate of spruce tree migration, it would jump three thousand years.

* * *

Anyway, Bob Marshall planted white spruce seeds from the Lake States Forest Experiment Station in Wisconsin on Barrenland and Kinnorutin creeks north of timber line in 1939.

He planted white spruce seeds north of timber line four months before he died. Just four months before his fatal heart attack at the age of thirty-eight, he planted the seeds north of timber line in the central Brooks Range.

* * *

I could find no record that anyone had followed up on Bob Marshall's experiment to test his theory. There was no record of anyone hiking into the range to see if the spruce seeds had grown.

In nearly thirty years no one had visited Robert Marshall's plantings, so I wrote to his brother, George, who had edited Bob's journals. George Marshall was then on the governing board of the Wilderness Society. I wanted to learn if he knew whether anyone had visited these plots.

So far as he knew, no one had returned to Bob Marshall's planting in the wilderness of the Brooks Range since his death in 1939.

* * *

This was the excuse I needed. This was it. My reason to go.

I had read of this great range which stretched over five hundred miles across the wildest and least known part of Alaska. I had read the journals of Bob Marshall, but like him had the notion that exploration should have a social justification. At that time I had this notion that a social justification was needed and here it was.

Yes, here it was. I was on a quest for Bob Marshall's trees. I was on a quest. That was my rationale. Actually, it was because I had never been there. Adventure!

*   *   *

So in August of 1966 I began my quest. With a student photographer from the graduate school where I was teaching, I started my quest.

Dave and I hiked over the mountains from isolated Chimney Pass Lake where a small bush plane on floats left us. We climbed over the mountains and up the Hammond River to Kinnorutin Creek. There Marshall had planted seeds the last summer he was here. I found no evidence that the seeds had sprouted.

There was no evidence that the spruce seeds had grown in his plots on Barrenland Creek either, which we reached after climbing over two passes beyond the confluence of the North Fork of the Koyokuk River and Alinement Creek.

In July of 1939 Bob Marshall had written in his journal:

> After lunch I repeated the experiment which I had tried with negative results nine years before — the experiment to test my theory that lack of time, not unfavorable conditions had prevented the further progress of the northern timber line. I had brought with me this time white spruce seeds which the Lakes Forest Experiment Station had provided. I marked two square plots on a flat about ten feet above the creek. On the larger one, 12 by 12 feet, I sowed the seeds directly among the sphagnum moss, *Dryas octopetala,* and dwarfed willow. On the

other plot, which was 8 by 8 feet, I scraped away the vegetation and sowed the seeds on mineral soil.

*   *   *

Although I found no evidence that Marshall's plant-ings had been successful on my trip in 1966, I still felt his theory was valid and planned to return in the future and replant in his original site on Barrenland Creek.

*   *   *

And so I did. Two years later the opportunity came when I included in my sabbatical study in human ecol-ogy the inland mountain Eskimos gathered in the village of Anaktuvuk Pass on top of the range.

Anaktuvuk Pass is the Eskimo's ancient campsite on the caribou migration route through the center of the Brooks Range. It is forty miles north of timber line and accessible today by aircraft.

My plan was to hike the forty or fifty miles from Anaktuvuk Pass along the top of the range to Barrenland Creek. However, I would have to detour south far enough to gather spruce seeds or seedlings.

I would have to detour, but nearly everyone has to detour when on a quest.

*   *   *

With my wife, Billie, as companion and photographer, we estimated the time and supplies needed for our trip into these rugged mountains. Carefully, we planned our trip before flying from Fairbanks to the Eskimo village in Anaktuvuk Pass.

During our stay in the village, it became evident that our hike through the rough terrain and over the passes to Barrenland Creek could be exceptionally difficult.

It became evident because I had not counted on high water in the rivers from early rains. I had not counted on high water and the mosquito hatches were unusually

heavy. Having hiked this wilderness before, I had no il-
lusions as to its hardship.

There is a difference between wading hip deep through
an icy stream and attempting to swim it. Yes there is.

*   *   *

While we were talking with one of our Eskimo hosts
about our concerns, he suggested that we discuss our
plans with the pilot of the mail plane to Anaktuvuk Pass.
The pilot was a big-game outfitter with a hunting campsite in the general area we wanted to visit.

It was a lucky contact. The pilot spread out a map
on the gravel of the Anaktuvuk Pass airstrip. We discovered a small lake on the summit of the range where
he felt he could land his small float plane. This would
deliver us to within eight air miles of the area of Bob
Marshall's plots on Barrenland Creek.

On the map it was only eight air miles but in the
precipitous canyon headwaters of the Koyokuk River it
meant more than twice that far on foot. It meant hiking over slopes usually traversed only by mountain sheep.

It also meant an additional hike of more than twelve
air miles south to timber line to collect seeds or seedlings, but compared to the hundred-mile backpack we
had planned, this trip seemed simple.

When what appears to be simple is compared to something more difficult, it seems simple. It always seems
simple when compared to something more difficult.

*   *   *

Anyway, we flew the three hundred miles back to Fairbanks to begin our trip.

Again we met good fortune. This was in the form of
one hundred four-year-old white spruce seedlings provided by the Forestry Sciences Laboratory at the University of Alaska.

We did not have to make the extra trip south of timber line to search out seeds or dig seedlings. It also guaranteed the age and quality of the trees we could plant provided we could get them into the range in good order.

*   *   *

Our bush pilot had warned us that it would be a crowded trip as he was provisioning his Dall sheep hunting camp.

When we arrived at the float pond in Fairbanks where his small plane was tied to a stake on the shore, I wondered how three people with several cartons of groceries, backpacks, rifles, a hundred spruce seedlings, two five gallon cans and a fifteen gallon barrel of gasoline were going to be squeezed aboard, much less get airborne.

Well, we filled every inch of space including our laps. I carried the precious seedlings on my lap. The floatplane taxied to the far end of the pond.

*   *   *

Using the full length of the pond to get airborne, we slowly rose toward the hills north of Fairbanks. We climbed steadily to six thousand feet. At six thousand feet we were over the Indian settlement of Stevens Village on the Yukon River one hundred miles north.

*   *   *

After another hundred miles, there ahead was the great blue range. Then we were above the mountains and over Chimney Peak and the small lake where I had been left two years before to begin my search for Bob Marshall's plots.

We made a turn over the saddle above the lake where we had photographed a grizzly bear, and then followed our route up the Hammond River and over Kinnorutin Pass. There we had climbed beneath Apoon Mountain's glacier. Our small plane then flew around the peak of Mount Doonerak's rocky crags and across the North Fork

of the Koyokuk River to drop down on a little lake shortly
before noon on top of the range.

*   *   *

We waded ashore.

With seedlings, backpacks, rifle and camera we waded
ashore. The pilot said he would pick us up in about five
days if the weather permitted. Have a good time, he said.
With a wave of his hand he again said, have a good time,
and took off toward the north.

*   *   *

In the silence, following the plane's disappearance,
Billie and I looked at each other and smiled.

We were here. Yes, here we were and I loaded the
rifle. Billie checked the camera. After tying our precious
cargo of trees on top of my pack we started across the
tussocks to our first crossing of the North Fork of the
Koyokuk River.

*   *   *

That evening I wrote in my journal:

. . . Sunday, August 4 . . . After wading the icy North
Fork, the walking was tedious through sedge and muskeg,
much too familiar from the 1966 hike into Anaktuvuk
Pass. Many birds — longspurs and horned larks — but the
only large animals were two Dall sheep on the slope to
the east. Made camp at the canyon mouth of the second
tributary south of Summit which I called *Nuliak Creek*
in honor of my companion (Nuliak is wife in Eskimo).
The sky is turning black with clouds and the wind has
picked up. With a caribou antler for a post, I put up a
tarp in front of the tent to keep the willow sticks dry
for a morning fire. . . .

*   *   *

Monday, August 5 . . . It was a good thing we prepared
for a wet camp as it rained all night and the wind blew
the tarp with a continual flapping. Low clouds reached

the ground this morning with a heavy mist falling, but no hard rain. The cardboard box of spruce tree seedlings has absorbed so much water it is disintegrating. It is necessary to wrap the box up net-like in nylon cord I carry for emergency use.

The clouds kept the mountain tops covered as we rimmed along beneath their ceiling. They broke once near the edge of a great cut before Barrenland Creek, and just above us a band of seventeen Dall sheep stood and watched while I took off my pack to wind the camera. They ran up the slope into the clouds, but not before we caught them on film.

By seven p.m., rimming up Barrenland Creek's north side, we looked down on the tree planting site where Bob Marshall's stakes still marked his plot after twenty-nine years of arctic freeze and break-up. Because the weather was unpredictable, I planted a few trees immediately. We wanted the site and planting recorded on film. The rain began again before the tent was fully up. We pitched it facing a large rock so the wind would not blow on our willow fire under the fly sheet. The storm soon became driving sleet mixed with rain.

All gear is where it will stay dry under the tarp, and we have arrived with our trees intact. As wind and rain buffet our tent, we talk of the inland Eskimos, who for thousands of years listened to the same sounds on their caribou skin shelters. There is a primeval quality of peace in this wilderness, a contentment at being warm in a snug tent, with a full stomach, a thick mattress of tundra beneath, a sense of accomplishment.

*   *   *

Tuesday, August 6 . . . It rained most of the night but was breaking up before we finished breakfast. Spent the day planting. Marshall's old site is about 100 yards upstream from the first main tributary entering Barrenland

Creek from the north. The location, as Bob described it on a flat about ten feet above the creek, refers to elevation. At present the location is about 100 feet north of Barrenland Creek. I built four rock corners around three-foot willow stakes to re-mark the plot, leaving Bob's markers as they were found. One of his two plots has washed out, only one willow stake remained at a corner. I thought it fitting to take it back to his brother, George, who in editing Bob's journals of exploration and mapping of this wilderness has come to know and love this land.

In order to protect the site from unintentional vandalism (as geology exploration by helicopter is no respecter of distance or rough terrain), I left the following inscription in both the northwest and southeast rock corners, placing one in a tobacco can and a copy in a peanut can.

NOTE: WITHIN THESE MARKERS ARE PLANTED 4-YEAR-OLD WHITE SPRUCE SEEDLINGS FROM FORESTRY SCIENCES LABORATORY, UNIVERSITY OF ALASKA, GIFT OF DR. LESLIE VIEREK. PLANTED AUGUST 6, 1968 BY SAM WRIGHT ON SITE OF PLANTING BY ROBERT MARSHALL. OLD MARKERS OF WILLOW — ROBERT MARSHALL'S ORIGINAL SITE MARKERS. THIS REPLANTING, A CONTINUING TEST OF BOB MARSHALL'S THEORY OF NORTHERN LIMIT OF SPRUCE GROWTH. PLEASE DO NOT DISTURB AND REPORT TO SAM WRIGHT, 2441 LECONTE AVE. BERKELEY, CALIFORNIA.

*   *   *

Now we were on our way back to the small lake on the summit of the pass to rendezvous with the bush plane. Billie and I stood watching the handsome ram on the promontory across the canyon of the North Fork with our field glasses. I thought how tragic it would be to lose this last great wilderness to the grind of road building equipment and the clutter of civilization. It would be a tragedy, but in the name of progress this seems to be the destiny of all wild places in our western world.

*   *   *

As we hoisted our packs and edged along the mountainside above the tumbling river, I made a pledge to myself. I made a pledge to do all I could to save this wilderness.

In replanting on this site, I had picked up the trail of Bob Marshall. And now we share another common goal — the preservation of these mountains — that there may remain on this continent a wild place where the song of wolves and the migration of caribou may remind us of who we are and from whence we came.

*   *   *

This pledge was not a light decision. We did not return to the San Francisco Bay Area at the end of the summer.

Instead, Billie and I moved into a 12-by-12-foot log cabin in the Brooks Range in early September, as I have already told about. We moved into the wilderness so we could speak on the ground for this last great wild place on the North American continent.

*   *   *

Although survey crews have mapped routes across the range for roads, oil pipelines and a railroad, the wilderness of the Brooks Range is still largely the land Robert Marshall knew.

History is not only in the past. It is what we do in the present.

At present, in the arctic wilderness north of timber line, there is now a small grove of seedlings which have jumped three thousand years.

His machines fill the earth with their thunder, but his heart is heavy within him. He has un- locked the force of the atom, but has not learned the might of his own spirit. Great are his skill and power, yet he lives in uncertainty and fear.

EDWIN C. PALMER

15
Pipe Dream
An afterthought on the trans-Alaska pipeline

It was called Alaska's answer to the energy shortage, the eight-hundred-mile nickel-plated trans-Alaska oil pipeline.

*　　*　　*

But the wilderness was raped. It will never again be the wilderness it was after being raped by a metal and fiberglass insulated pipe twisting through the Brooks Range and across miles of tundra with its gravel haul road beside it.

*　　*　　*

It is the haul road more than oil which is destroying the wilderness. It is not the oil, which makes plastic bottles and TV cases in Korea and Japan; it is the road which returns the plastic and ATVs. All-terrain-vehicles are already vandalizing the north.

It is the bridge across the Yukon River and the people who cross the bridge because the bridge is there.

Because the bridge is there people cross it and bring their plastic and civilization. Because there is a bridge across the Yukon and a road across the mountains and a road across the tundra to the oil fields on the arctic coast, the wilderness is in jeopardy.

Now there is a road to bring civilization and progress to the wilderness, so God bless us. Yes, God bless us all.

*   *   *

For eight months I was a counselor in construction camps north of the Yukon. I was a counselor between the Prudhoe Bay oil fields and the Yukon River, from Franklin Bluffs and Happy Valley to Coldfoot and Prospect Creek camps. Billie and I were both counselors on the trans-Alaska pipeline project.

We were called site-counselors because we were on the construction site where counselors should be to counsel, and we gave counsel. We gave counsel to engineers about drunk Indians and counsel to Eskimos about drunk engineers and counsel to women about men and counsel to truck drivers about security guards and counsel to Texans about Alaskans and counsel to atheistic Protestants about visiting orthodox Jewish chaplains and we counseled everyone about the wilderness because we were all in the wilderness.

However, the wilderness of the Brooks Range was not the wilderness that needed our counsel. It was the wilderness of the construction project. Yes, the construction project.

*   *   *

There we were, only a short helicopter flight from Koviashuvik.

There we were, working seven days a week on twenty-four hour call. Working for the Alyeska Pipeline Service Company, working to get its job done as quickly and effectively as possible, working to get the construction project out of the wilderness, working for money so we would have a grubstake to stay in the wilderness, working for money.

Like everybody else we were working for money.

*　　*　　*

We found it funny that we were working for money. It was funny because it takes money not to work for money.

Like everyone on the pipeline project, we were not really working for money, we were working for dreams.

We were all working for dreams, pipe dreams, for money and dreams.

*　　*　　*

Pat Parmley had a dream of an island off the coast of Belize where he and his wife, Elizabeth, would retire. On the tropical beach of their island they would no longer work for money. They made a down-payment on their island and they were working twelve-hour night shifts in Coldfoot and Dietrich camps for their dream.

Okitkun had a dream to return to his village to hunt and fish, like in the old days.

Alexandra Atchak had a dream. And so did the welder's helper who was flown out on a medivac to a psychiatric institution in Anchorage. And the side-boom operator had a dream before he was crushed by a cave-in. And Mary Lou and Harley, and Killbear and Dean Elston all had dreams.

I wonder do they still have their dreams?

Billie and I have our dream of Koviashuvik but dreams change. Yes, they do.

*　　*　　*

I have a dream, Martin Luther King, Junior said through the loudspeakers the day we marched in front

of the Washington Monument and sang "We Shall Over-
come," and I sat on the grass in the sun with thousands
of others. I too had a dream.

I did not know it was Koviashuvik. I did not know
about Koviashuvik because I did not know Eskimo and
had never been in Alaska. I seldom thought of Alaska.
At least never thought of living in the Brooks Range,
but here I am and I still have a dream.

* * *

Anyway, we worked on the pipeline and I learned that
a dream is not a wish for what might be some day. No,
a dream is an exciting whisper answering the monotony
of days of dull routine.

A dream is not an outward thing taking its form only
from the environment in which it functions. It lives deep
within.

* * *

At Koviashuvik we still live our dream. But the Parm-
leys' island was sold to someone else and instead of tropical Belize they bought a liquor store in Homer, Alaska.
Okitkun developed ulcers and was sent to the native
hospital in Anchorage. Billie and I went home to Koviashuvik in the wilderness of the Brooks Range, but it was
not the wilderness it was because it had been raped by
a fiberglass insulated pipe.

* * *

Even so, we still live our dream. We still keep alive
the exciting whisper. Although our wilderness has been
changed we still have our dream.

16
Bless the Indians
A *theological journey in time and place*

Billie and I left in our nineteen-sixty-eight Volkswagen camper to visit the Indians on Friday the thirteenth. It was May.

From our home in Pleasant Valley we wound up the dirt road of Cherry Creek Hill to the Mogollon Rim, seven thousand feet above sea level. We were on our way to visit the Pueblo Indians in New Mexico.

* * *

I was born in New Mexico. I am a native like the Indians we were on our way to visit.

But not really like the Indians at Zuni or Jemez pueblos. Their ancestors were in New Mexico when my ancestors were on another continent. Our ancestors are different. Theirs were living in peace in the Southwest that we now share. Mine were warring in northern Europe.

I am glad we are not our ancestors although a lot of us would like to have been. If I had been, I would rather have been an Anasazi Indian in Frijoles Canyon in New Mexico.

*   *   *

We visited a good many of these pueblos. They are all well built with straight, well squared walls. Their towns have no definite streets. Their houses are three, five, six and even seven stories high, with many windows and terraces. The men spin and weave and the women cook, build houses, and keep them in good repair. They dress in garments of cotton cloth, and the women wear beautiful shawls of many colors. They are quiet, peaceful people of good appearance and excellent physique, alert and intelligent. They are not known to drink, a good omen indeed. We saw no maimed or deformed people among them. The men and women alike are excellent swimmers. They are also expert in the art of painting, and are good fishermen. They live in complete equality, neither exercising authority nor demanding obedience.

GASPAR PEREZ DE VILLAGAS, 1610

*   *   *

We filled our camper's tank with gasoline in Holbrook, Arizona.

We would not have stopped in Holbrook unless we needed gas because there is nothing in Holbrook that interests us. In some ways, Holbrook is not anywhere. It was a water-stop for the Santa Fe Railroad and now it is a gasoline stop for us on our way to Zuni.

*   *   *

Zuni pueblo is something else.

It was the last stop for Estevan, the first black man to visit the pueblo with Fray Marcos de Niza's expedition of 1539. He was arrogant and they killed him.

After hearing of Estevan's death, de Niza went only far enough to glimpse the Zuni pueblo before heading back to Mexico to announce that he had found the Kingdom of Cibola.

Fray Marcos de Niza was a liar. But because he was a priest Francisco Coronado believed him. Yes, Coronado believed that Zuni was the mythical province of the seven cities of Cibola which reportedly held the treasure of Montezuma. So he led an expedition to attack and capture the Zunis and discovered that de Niza's report was a hoax.

*   *   *

Anyway, the Franciscans built a mission there. In 1629 they built a mission which the Zunis did not like, so they left the mission in 1632 after the killing of two friars.

By 1629 the Zunis had learned how to tolerate the Catholic Church. And to this day they tolerate it, but the Kiva remains and Kachina dances and the Shalako Ceremony continue as ever.

We like the Zuni.

The people in Zuni still know they are A'shivi, which is what they call themselves in their own language. It means "the flesh."

*   *   *

From Zuni pueblo we drove on to spend the night camping among piñon trees where we could look out at the towering white sandstone cliff of El Morro. El Morro is a National Monument.

*   *   *

In the morning there they were. There were the names. Yes, the names of Spaniards, by their own hand, carved in the base of sandstone cliffs more than a hundred years before George Washington was elected our first president.

And before the Spaniards, long before the Spaniards,

the Anasazi left their pictographs. They were there with the names of others who through the years camped by this water-hole at the base of towering El Morro. In 1906 it was set aside as a National Monument and no more graffiti allowed.

However, the cliff swallows don't know this. They still make their mark with mud nests and swoop for insects above the water-hole and ride updrafts against the giant bluff into a clear blue sky.

We drove on to Acoma pueblo, a city in the sky.

*　　*　　*

On top of a mesa 365 feet above the surrounding valley, the people of the white rock have lived for the past thousand years.

Acoma is the native word meaning people of the white rock. It was not until 1540 that the first European, a Captain Hernando de Alvarado, arrived. He was the first.

Then came the Zaldivars, and in 1599 during a three day battle hundreds of Indians were killed by the Spaniards, the town destroyed. The women were sentenced to 20 years labor and the male captives sentenced the same. Yes, sentenced the same but in addition had one foot chopped off.

Young boys were given to Vincente de Zaldivar as a reward for his victory and the young girls given to the church.

The impressive mission church, rebuilt many times but still dominating the pueblo today, was originally built by forced labor in the name of Christ. In the name of Christ most of the churches in the pueblos were first built by forced labor.

Anyway, the people of Acoma still hold their ancient ceremonies in the pueblo in the sky and now charge admission to visit their city or take pictures.

*　　*　　*

I had last visited Acoma in 1944.

I was in graduate school at the University of New Mexico in Albuquerque and an Indian classmate of mine and I climbed Enchanted Mesa to verify the remains of ruins on its top. Enchanted Mesa, even more dramatic than Acoma, reaches high above the valley and we could look out across at the sky city and hear the drum-beat of the harvest dance and fiesta.

Below us a red-tailed hawk soared in a rising thermal and the drum-beats from the pueblo matched my pulse after the strenuous climb. In that moment I knew what it was to be Acoma.

Today, as we watched the sky-city bus drive from the new exhibit center up the steep paved road with its load of tourists, I wondered.

*   *   *

But there was Enchanted Mesa still sheer and white in the spring sunshine. There it was with no mission on top and only the ancient hand and foot-holds up its cliff.

Again, a red-tailed hawk soared out. This time it soared against the sky above us, and again I heard the drum-beat of my heart.

Again, I knew.

*   *   *

Then we drove through the pueblos of Laguna and Santa Ana on our way to Jemez.

*   *   *

Laguna is not an old pueblo.

It is not as old as Zuni or Acoma or any of the others we visited. It was founded in 1699 by Indians from Santo Domingo and Cochiti who survived the Diego Vargas attack on their stronghold in 1694.

In 1680 the Indians revolted. All the tribes united

to drive out the invaders. For the first time in their history they united and drove the Spaniards out.

At least as far as El Paso, they drove the Spaniards out for twelve years until General Diego Vargas marched north with his army in 1693 and began re-establishing Spanish authority in New Mexico.

He did not establish authority in Laguna however until 1699, and by then the Indians from Acoma, Zuni, Oraibi, Zia, San Felipe, Sandia and Jemez had joined those of other pueblos. Even today the clans at Laguna trace their origins to at least nine other pueblos.

*   *   *

Unlike Laguna, Santa Ana was an established pueblo before the Spaniards came. It was called Tamata, but in 1598 Juan de Onate renamed it Saint Anne.

After the Indians drove the Spanish from their territory in 1680, Pedro de Posada, governor of El Paso, led an attack on Santa Ana in 1687 and burned the village. He burned the village and those who escaped united with the survivors of Zia pueblo to establish a new village on Red Mesa near Jemez.

Later they returned. They returned to Santa Ana and rebuilt the village in 1692 under the Spanish rule of General Diego de Vargas.

*   *   *

Today there are not many people left in the pueblo, but in 1944 during the Green Corn Dance in July, the pueblo was crowded with Indians and visitors.

Santa Ana pottery was in great demand then and the fiesta was as gay as any I have attended. It was gay with bright blankets and the people danced and the rains came and it was as if the Spanish had never come, except the mission dominated the pueblo and the wooden cross on the adobe bell-tower stood out against a blue sky.

In 1944 the drums beat and moccasin feet called to mother earth to grow the corn and the beans and squash for a country at war. We were at war and there were Indians in army uniform and some danced in uniform, but it was not strange to me, their being in uniform.

Now it would be strange, but it wasn't then. The cross on the mission seemed strange to me then. It does even now.

*   *   *

We did not stop in Zia on our way to Jemez. Zia is known for the fine polychrome pottery made there.

Even today, the inhabitants of Zia are regarded as social outcasts by many other pueblos because of their alliance with the Spaniards in 1692, when they joined in the attack on other pueblos.

This is not why we by-passed Zia. We wanted to spend the night along the Jemez River. Billie and I do not hold 396-year-old grudges. Pueblo Indians have long memories.

*   *   *

At Jemez pueblo they refer to themselves as "Jemez People" and call their pueblo Walatowa, which means "the people in the canyon." And what a fantastic canyon it is.

From Redondo Peak, which thrusts 11,254 feet above sea level, the melting winter snows and numerous springs feed the rushing stream of the Jemez River between towering cliffs. In the protected canyon the Jemez people cultivated, as they still do, the sacred triad of squash, beans and maize.

*   *   *

Today we call maize corn but corn is an English word for any edible grain, especially wheat in England and oats in Scotland.

Maize was called Indian corn in colonial New England,

and corn with varied colored kernels is still referred to as Indian corn in seed catalogues. Maize originated in the Andes Mountains and was developed by the Indians. Yes, the corn we know was created by the Indians.

Corn cannot reseed itself. If we disappear, maize disappears. To the people of the pueblos maize was sacred. It still is. It had better be sacred to us all. It needs us.

*   *   *

Anyway, Billie and I drove into Jemez pueblo with its red clay dome-shaped ovens.

Behind each adobe dwelling there are ovens for baking in every pueblo. Even when modern kitchens with gas and electricity have been added to village homes, baking is still done in outdoor ovens.

Tourists call them beehive ovens but only in children's fairy tale books have I seen the straw beehives shaped like these ovens.

Beehives are square boxes today. Today beehives are wooden boxes. I don't know anyone who has seen a real straw beehive shaped like a pueblo oven. If I saw a straw beehive in a story book, I would say its shape was oven-shaped. I would call it an oven beehive.

*   *   *

In 1541, when this Towa-speaking tribe was first contacted by the Spaniards, they were living in eleven small villages. The Spaniards concentrated them into two villages where they built missions.

From the earliest time the Jemez had a hostile attitude toward the Spaniards. They did not like the authority of the Spanish and two unsuccessful uprisings against the Spanish authority occurred before the Pueblo rebellion of 1680.

*   *   *

When the Spanish tried to re-conquer Jemez, the Indians retreated to fortified positions on mesa tops above the canyon whenever soldiers appeared. According to the Spanish chroniclers, Jemez sent out raiding parties from these strongholds to harass Zia and Santa Ana pueblos for remaining loyal to the Spaniards.

*   *   *

Anyway, the Jemez held out until 1694, when de Vargas with the help of Zia and Santa Ana allies destroyed their mesa-top strongholds.

The survivors resettled in the canyon but not for long. The Jemez enlisted aid from Zuni and Acoma and even from some Navajo tribes and resumed their hostilities against the Spanish-controlled pueblos to the south.

Well anyway, by 1703 Spanish power dominated, and most of the people returned to Jemez valley and built their present village where they had once lived before the Spanish arrived.

They built this pueblo where the mission and the Kiva still face each other in the Plaza. The mission faces the Kiva, the Indians' sacred underground meeting place. But the Kiva is round and faces everywhere, even up and down.

To this day the Kiva faces everywhere. The round Kiva of the pueblo faces everywhere.

*   *   *

Harmony with the natural world is the religious conviction of Pueblo Indians, and harmony must also be maintained in family, clan and societal relationships. Even today the welfare of the group ranks before the individual.

*   *   *

The Catholic church has claimed converts here for over 300 years but the native religion has not diminished.

Even though they participate in baptism, confirmation, marriage and burial ceremonies of the church the importance of the native religion has not diminished.

Today the Indians make use of both religious systems. Although these religions are different and separate, and even though their world views are in contrast, the Indians find no inconsistency in making use of both.

*   *   *

That we must live in harmony with the world around us is a belief so strong among the Pueblos that it is not possible to separate religion from everyday life.

Dances and ceremonies performed throughout the year are enactments of this philosophy. The fact that these tribal groups have not only survived 400 years of occupation by alien cultures, but have maintained more of their native life than they have lost, is a great testament to a world view and way of life we dare not dismiss. Particularly in today's ethnocentric world where we are eager to teach but reluctant to learn.

*   *   *

We drove up the canyon and camped for the night next to the swollen Jemez River under new-leafed cottonwood trees.

*   *   *

First light of the sun bounced off red cliffs a thousand feet above us as I heated breakfast water on our propane stove.

A robin singing his territorial song in the cottonwoods was soon matched by a canyon wren's rushing cadence down the scale from the Pilgrims' Chorus in *Tannhauser*. The canyon wren's ancestors were no doubt singing their cadence here long before Richard Wagner wrote his composition. Centuries ago Jemez Indians heard the song and watched the morning sun creep down the canyon wall even as I watched it on this clear spring morning.

Then I opened the camper door and gave Billie her wake-up cup of coffee.

Before the sun reached us down by the river, we were on our way over the mountain passes to Frijoles Canyon in Bandelier National Monument.

*   *   *

Frijoles Canyon is where ancestors of the pueblos lived before the Spaniards came. In Frijoles Canyon the ruins of an ancient village have been excavated, the round Kiva fits the ancient plaza built 800 years ago. In the pueblos today it still fits.

*   *   *

We then drove into Los Alamos where nothing fits. Depending upon your point of view, nothing fits.

I had not been in Los Alamos for thirty-seven years and here I was back again in a strange village, built since I was here during World War II.

In this secret hideaway they were putting together Trinity. They were putting together a device that would change the world. And it did. At Alamogordo, Hiroshima and Nagasaki it changed the world.

After being held up in traffic by Christians on their way to church we had breakfast at McDonald's. We had breakfast in Los Alamos on Sunday morning at mission McDonald's which replaced the cross with golden arches.

*   *   *

Back in 1945 Los Alamos did not fit the landscape with its new buildings. They did not fit but they were few and we were at war and nothing fits when the world is at war.

It was strange and exciting then but mostly strange in 1944 and 1945 when Los Alamos was a secret place and we called it site Y.

We called it site Y and I drove up from site T in Albuquerque through Santa Fe to cross the Rio Grande River at San Ildefonso pueblo and then climbed the mountain to be checked through a guarded gate among the ponderosa pines.

It was strange then, but not as strange as Los Alamos is today with traffic lights and supermarkets, chain stores and great metallic factory buildings. At least they look like factory buildings even though they are called laboratories because Ph.D.s work in laboratories not factories.

      *   *   *

Today Los Alamos is a strange and alien growth on the mountain slopes below Redondo Peak. It does not fit. To me it does not fit, like the golden arches of McDonald's fast food stop would not fit in the plaza of San Ildefonso pueblo.

      *   *   *

The San Ildefonso Indians, on the banks of the Rio Grande River below Los Alamos, have inhabited this area from about 1300 A.D.

In 1598 when Onate visited the village it was located about a mile from the present pueblo. When the Indians took part in the rebellion of 1680 they destroyed the mission and village and moved to the top of Black Mesa.

On nearby Black Mesa, with allies from other neighboring tribes, they held out for nine months against de Vargas' soldiers. They withstood three assaults before they surrendered and returned to the valley.

Then they revolted again against Spanish authority. In 1696 they revolted and abandoned their pueblo to find refuge with other tribes. Some moved as far away as the Hopi village of Oraibi in northern Arizona.

      *   *   *

Anyway, San Ildefonso is famous for its polished black pottery which is a revival of an earlier style found in Indian ruins on the Pajarito Plateau.

In 1919 Maria Martinez and her husband Julian began making polished ware with matte black designs and today Maria Martinez is the most famous of all Indian potters. If you have one of her originals, you are fortunate. Yes you are.

Then in 1931 Rosalie Aguilar produced the first carved pots. Since then a number of excellent potters continue to make fine polished black and red ware using both matte and carving decorative techniques.

*   *   *

Not far up the Rio Grande River is the pueblo of Santa Clara, also famous for its polished black pottery. Santa Clara potters like those of San Ildefonso are world renowned.

Both Santa Clara and San Ildefonso Indians speak the Tewa language, and according to their tradition the Tewas emerged from a small opening in the earth in what is now Colorado. One tradition is that the cliff dwellings of Mesa Verde are the ancestral homes of the Santa Clara and San Ildefonso tribes.

Anyway, Santa Clara was built in the 14th century and the Spaniards arrived 300 years later and in 1620 established a church in the village.

Following the 1680 rebellion, the Santa Clarans joined other Tewas in the fortress on Black Mesa and after its surrender to troops of General de Vargas some of them moved west to become residents of Zuni. Others moved even farther west to the Hopi villages in Arizona.

After the reconquest of New Mexico by the Spaniards many Santa Clarans moved back to re-occupy the pueblo.

Today many Santa Clarans are employed at Los Alamos. So are San Ildefonsans. So are hundreds of physicists who still see the Pueblo Indians as undeveloped Americans.

* * *

On our way up the Rio Grande River to Taos pueblo is the village of San Juan, where in 1598 the first capital of New Mexico was established by Don Juan de Onate.

The next year the capital was moved across the river to the village of Yunqueyunque which means "the ravine village" in Tewa. The people living in Yunqueyunque voluntarily gave up their village to the Spaniards and took up residence in San Juan, where the Spaniards were so impressed by the hospitality of these people that they named the pueblo San Juan De Los Caballeros.

This was before the harshness of Spanish rule and religion reached a peak in 1675 when 47 Indian leaders from a number of pueblos were whipped for practicing witchcraft.

Anyway, a medicine man from San Juan was one of the leaders whipped. This was a mistake for the Spaniards. It was a mistake because it was this religious leader, Popé, who later conceived, organized and led the pueblo rebellion of 1680. He led the rebellion which drove the Spanish from the Rio Grande Valley, the only time the pueblos before or since united to achieve a common goal.

* * *

I wish that Yunqueyunque had remained the capital of New Mexico instead of the Spaniards moving it south to Santa Fe.

Later history might have been different as the wagon masters headed west on the "Trail to Yunqueyunque."

The railroad across the west would be called the Yunqueyunque Railroad, and the Sons of the Pioneers would have sung "On the Yunqueyunque Trail."

Maybe history would have been different if old Yun-queyunque had remained the capital. I like to think so.

*   *   *

Anyway, we drove north along the river gorge of the Rio Grande to Taos.

Taos is the most northern living pueblo where the Plains Indians met to trade bison meat and hides for pueblo maize and textiles before the coming of the Spaniards.

Taos was first visited by Alvarado in 1540. A hundred years later the village was abandoned in reaction to Spanish rule and the people moved to the plains with the Jicarilla Apaches. Two years later they were brought back by the Spaniards in 1642.

Again, the Spaniards made a mistake because Taos became the base of operations for the conspirators who planned the pueblo rebellion of 1680. On August 10th of that year the Spanish priests and settlers in Taos were killed and Taos joined the other pueblos in attacking Santa Fe and driving the Spanish south to El Paso.

*   *   *

Today, Taos pueblo with its multistoried construction and surrounding adobe wall is a showplace for tourists. A fee is now charged to enter the village and no checks or credit cards are honored. Not yet.

*   *   *

Outside the pueblo, the town of Taos is no longer the sleepy village I knew in the 1940s. Like Los Alamos, it no longer fits. Neither did we fit in the town of Taos, so we headed south and camped off an isolated road among the junipers beyond Santa Fe.

Two coyotes, a jackrabbit and a red-tailed hawk were mildly disturbed by our presence on the mesa.

Except for lights of the pueblos of San Felipe and

Santo Domingo along the river in the distance below us, and the headlights of traffic on Interstate 25 between Santa Fe and Albuquerque, it was like it was before the Europeans arrived.

Not really.

No, it will never be again.

*   *   *

We drove through the campus of the University of New Mexico in Albuquerque where I received a Bachelor of Science degree and had a Teaching Fellowship in Botany and Zoology in the 1940s.

In the 1940s the world was at war and I was recruited by the Office of Scientific Research and Development into secret projects which included the Manhattan Project. This was the most dramatic because it made a big bang at Alamogordo, then at Hiroshima and Nagasaki.

A big bang today would be the beginning of the end of us all.

*   *   *

The beginning of the end might have been the bang we made near Alamogordo. I think so but hope not.

It was called Trinity. Trinity is a Christian term for Father, Son and Holy Ghost.

*   *   *

We drove to my old address in Albuquerque to see the first house I'd ever owned but it was gone. The house was gone and in its place was a new fundamentalist Bible Church. So much for Trinity.

*   *   *

Then we visited Isleta, the Indian pueblo south of Albuquerque first described by the Spanish in 1540.

Today, the church of San Antonio de la Isleta dominates the plaza and though it has been rebuilt and remodeled many times it still includes portions of the original mission of San Agustin de la Isleta built in 1626.

Following the rebellion of 1680 Isleta was attacked by the Spaniards in their attempt to reconquer New Mexico, and hundreds of captives from Isleta pueblo were settled in a new village south of El Paso called Isleta del Sur.

It is still there. Those Isletans never returned.

*   *   *

Most of the pueblos we visited are still living communities but not all.

In Frijoles Canyon, at Bandelier National Monument, only ruins remain of the ancient village.

Another ancient ruin we visited was Kuaua, on the terrace bank of the Rio Grande River west of Bernallio, New Mexico. In 1583 Antonio Espejo mentions Kuaua. He spells it Guagua in Spanish:

> . . . from each pueblo people came out to receive us, taking us to their pueblos and giving us a great quantity of turkeys, maize, beans, tortillas and other kinds of bread . . . they grind on very large stones. Five or six women together grind raw corn . . . and from this flour they make different kinds of bread . . . In each plaza of the towns they have two estufas [Kivas] which are houses built underground, very well sheltered and closed with seats of stone against the walls to sit on. Likewise they have at the door of each estufa a ladder on which to descend . . .

*   *   *

Something must have happened at that time to alienate these Rio Grande Indians, for later in June of that year, after visiting pueblos to the west including Acoma and Zuni, the Espejo party returned to the Rio Grande where they found the Indians hostile. Most of them left the villages when the Spaniards returned, and those who remained jeered at the Spaniards.

Diego Perez de Luxan, who accompanied Espejo, writes of the village of Puala on the east bank of the Rio Grande where there were some 30 Indians on top of their houses. The Spaniards requested food but the Indians mocked them. Luxan wrote:

> . . . the corners of the pueblo were taken by four men and four others with two servants began to seize those they could lay hands on. We put them in an estufa. And as the pueblo was large and some had hidden themselves there we set fire to the big pueblo of Puala where we thought some were burned to death because of the cries they uttered. We at once took out the prisoners two at a time and lined them up against some poplars close to the pueblo of Puala and they were garroted and shot many times until they died. Sixteen were executed not counting those who burned to death. Some who did not seem to belong to Puala were set free. This was a strange deed for so few people in the midst of so many enemies.

*   *   *

From the Spanish accounts it is easy to see why the Indians rebelled in 1680.

*   *   *

Back to the ruin of Kuaua, in which excavation was begun in 1934 by the School of American Research, the Museum of New Mexico and the University of New Mexico. The excavation had the assistance of the Federal Relief Administration which supplied funds for laborers because it was the time of the Great Depression.

If it were not for the depression and the Federal Relief Administration the excavation of Kuaua might not have begun.

Anyway, the excavation of Kuaua was important

because one day in February 1935 a shovel full of dirt was thrown into a wheelbarrow from a test trench that had fragments of plaster with flecks of color. It was the flecks of color that caught attention.

*   *   *

The chamber was excavated and proved to be a ceremonial Kiva eighteen feet square and eight feet deep whose walls had been painted with murals centuries before contact with Europeans.

The preservation of these murals was a fantastic task and I had hoped to see the originals some day at the Museum of New Mexico in Sana Fe where they were stored. In Bertha Dutton's book, *Sun Father's Way, The Kiva Murals Of Kuaua* (University of New Mexico Press 1963), are pictures of the paintings. But I wanted to see the originals.

*   *   *

And here they were.

Here were the original paintings returned to Kuaua and recently put on display in a special room protected by glass. Yes, here they were with the original brush strokes of the medicine man as he did them more than 700 years ago. Here were pictures of the pueblo people's universe. Their symbolic gods or messengers of rain, lightning, fire, corn and other personalities of their tradition. Here were paintings that pre-dated any European contact and whose value is beyond price.

I felt more privileged to see these religious mural paintings than the hundreds I've visited in great museums around the world.

These spirits of the Anasazi are needed today. Yes they are.

*   *   *

And now we are on our way back across the Plains of San Augustin of New Mexico to our rock hogan in Pleasant Valley, Arizona.

On our left are twenty-seven great dish-shaped radio telescope antennas looking at the sky. This giant radio camera called the Very Large Array, or VLA, was constructed on this arid plain away from the interference of civilization's busyness and power lines to listen and watch beyond our galaxy.

Although it can see much farther, I am told that VLA is primarily watching an enigmatic object 13,000 light years away called SS433, and that SS433 is the most famous neutron-star flasher in our galaxy.

It is famous because we don't understand it. Some feel it important that we do. Unlike astronomy, when it comes to people and cultures we are ethnocentric, still eager to teach but reluctant to learn.

*   *   *

Did we learn anything on our trip to the pueblos?

As we drove along the Mogollon Rim into a scarlet sky before winding into Pleasant Valley, I remembered the Zuni saying recorded by Frank H. Cushing, who lived with them in the 1880s. He spoke their language and was initiated into the Bow priesthood after being adopted into the Pitchikwe clan.

> Five things alone are necessary to the sustenance and comfort of the dark ones, the Indians, among the children of earth:
>
> > The sun, who is the Father of all.
> > The earth, who is the Mother.
> > The water, who is the Grandfather.
> > The fire, who is the Grandmother.
> > Our brothers and sisters the corn,
> >   and seeds and growing things.

To these I would add The Spirit of Care among people, all the people, in a beautiful world we did not create but which sustains us in the vastness of infinite time and space.

*   *   *

Bless the Indians. Yes, bless the Indians and may their gods bless us all.

Beloved Pan, and all ye other gods
who haunt this place, give me
beauty in the inward soul; and
may the outward and inward man
be at one. May I reckon the wise
to be the wealthy, and may I have
such a quantity of gold as none
but the temperate can carry.

PLATO 428–348B.C.
Prayer of Socrates, *Phaedrus*

17
Koviashuktok

An Eskimo perspective

Now I want to tell something about my first journey in Alaska. About my meeting with the inland mountain Eskimos who are our neighbors. Although they live over a hundred air miles from Koviashuvik in Anaktuvuk Pass, they are our neighbors. Yes, neighbors.

*   *   *

With a graduate student who accompanied me as photographer, I hiked through the trailless mountains of the Brooks Range for ten days. A bush pilot had flown us into the range in his float plane and let us out on the shore of a small lake.

We hiked over mountain passes for ten days until we crossed the foothills of Three River Mountain in the center of the Brooks Range. There below us was our destination, the Eskimo village in Anaktuvuk Pass.

*   *   *

The Eskimo village was a scattering of tents and sod huts. Two dozen huts and tents were dominated by a sheet-metal building. On a hill above the village was a log cabin with a small wooden cross above the door. I recognized the metal building as a school house with its predominant flagpole in front. The cabin on the hill was obviously a church.

*   *   *

I could see people through my field glasses. I watched a lone man walking toward the village from the mountains beyond the pass. He was wearing a fur-fringed parka and carrying a rifle. He also carried what appeared to be a skin bag slung across his back.

Children were playing by a crude foot-bridge which crossed the river between us and the village. The foot-bridge was a welcome site. To us it was a most welcome sight after days of wading icy steams. We were glad to arrive where a bush pilot could pick us up. But the most welcome site at the moment was that foot-bridge.

*   *   *

Before we arrived at the bridge, children spotted us and five boys ten to twelve years old came running toward us through the waist-high willows.

"Hello," they shouted. "Hello, what is your name?"

They unselfconsciously took our hands and repeated our names. We asked them theirs.

Then several men greeted us. They invited us into a dwelling where we stepped through a caribou-skin covered opening into a warm, dark room. The house was a single room of tundra-sod walls braced by poles, with a center pole supporting the turf roof.

To the right of the doorway as we entered was an iron stove. It was an oblong sheet-iron stove, raised from the dirt floor on tin cans. It glowed with a fire of green willow sticks. The open front glowed with a friendly warmth. We were not treated as strangers. We had no sense of strangeness in meeting these friendly people.

* * *

Two little girls, sitting on an old sleeping bag in a corner with a caribou skin pulled over their legs, greeted us with smiles. Our host, Thomas Rulland, introduced his wife, Ruth. She then made coffee which we all shared and during the following days we spent hours in tents and huts of most of the families in the pass.

When the bush pilot flew in to take us out, it was not easy to say goodbye. It was like a farewell to friends of many years. From these people I learned that friendship has little to do with length of time.

* * *

This experience in 1966 played a large part in my return to this Eskimo village at the crest of the Brooks Range two years later. Two years later I returned with Billie.

We returned to Anaktuvuk Pass as part of my sabbatical year value study. I had planned to hike from here for my experimental tree planting north of timber line, and by the coming winter we had settled into our own home in the wilderness of the Brooks Range to explore a way of life called Eskimo.

* * *

Since then, in the intervening years since I first visited Anaktuvuk Pass, much has happened to change a way of life these Eskimos have lived for centuries.

Their transportation for winter hunting and trapping was a dogsled. In 1966, it was still the dog team and sled. Today snowmobiles have replaced the dogs.

During my second visit in 1968, enterprising old Kakinya had arranged for a disassembled pool table to be flown

in. It was purchased through a mail-order house. He placed
it in a new, white canvas tent and opened the first pool
hall in Anaktuvuk Pass. On the pliant tundra, the pool
table had to be leveled frequently and the players had
to be careful not to punch holes in the canvas wall with
a cue stick.

That summer the 10-by-12-foot pool hall was a gathering place for the young men of the village.

*   *   *

However, the most dramatic change came the following year, in February. It was in the winter dark of 1969
that a youngster ran shouting through the village.

In the dark of winter he ran shouting, "Tractor coming, tractor coming!"

The shout was taken up by others and within an hour
the whole village was out to meet a great snow-cat-train
loaded with mobile camp equipment on its way to the
oil fields of Prudhoe Bay.

The village in Anaktuvuk Pass, whose contact with
Fairbanks 280 miles south had been by air, was now joined
to the road system of Alaska by a winter haul road through
the Brooks Range. Now it was joined to the Alaska road
system. The haul road's purpose was to bring equipment
to the oil fields at Prudhoe Bay on the Arctic coast, but
it brought the outside world to Anaktuvuk Pass.

All the problems of the modern world came into this
small village of inland Eskimos, still dependent on migrating herds of caribou. This was the beginning of the
end of a way of life which had sustained the Nunamiut
for thousands of years.

*   *   *

Out of these thousands of years, I heard an echo of
something important in the lives of these friends in
Anaktuvuk Pass. It was this echo that brought me back

to the wilderness north of the Arctic Circle. It still brings Billie and me back to our home at Koviashuvik.

* * *

Now listen to this.

Only in solitude, say the Eskimos, can a person find wisdom. Only in solitude can wisdom be found.

Since we wanted to learn the secret of their sense of at-homeness and the affirmative quality in their lives which made itself felt to all who came in contact with them, we asked what they called it.

They said it was koviashuktok.

* * *

Koviashuktok, to a categorizer or dictionary-maker, might be defined by such words as joy, happiness, elation, courage, understanding or perspective. But to categorize is in itself at odds with the quality implied in Koviashuktok. To categorize is inimical to Koviashuktok because the Eskimo language is not one which simply names things that already exist. It brings into being. It brings things into being as they are spoken.

I'll try to explain.

All Eskimo words are in effect forms of the verb to be which itself is lacking in Eskimo.

This is why it is said that there are a thousand words for snow in the Eskimo language. Actually, the words for snow or anything else are unlimited because snow never exists in itself but takes form from the action in which it participates. Snow is either falling, blowing, drifting, mixed with water, on clothes, being snowshoed upon, hard or soft, with distinctions only experienced in a meaningful context.

Whatever exists, the Eskimo shares in bringing into being whatever it is. With each act and statement the world is created, is brought into being, and each act accomplished is as quickly lost.

Everything is in context. Including the individual, everything is in context. There is nothing passive in relationship with the world because it is the person who reveals form. With an individual person creation becomes.

*   *   *

Like many others, when I think of the concerns of our time I think of the possibility of nuclear war.

I am aware that this is only a symptom. Although its possibility is real, it is only a symptom, like the destruction of plant and animal habitats of soil, water and air are symptoms. These are only symptoms of underlying habits of thought we have called common sense, but which no longer make sense because their premises are based in another age.

We are in a crisis of mind today. For this reason our whole way of seeing and thinking has to be explored. Our way of seeing and thinking has to be renovated. This is what I learned from Eskimos. We need to see and think in a new way. We need to think in a way that includes a larger context.

*   *   *

But back to a particular tent in Anaktuvuk Pass before the beginning of the end. Before our modern world rolled into this small Eskimo village with its worship of money and irrational religion, with a history of political revolutions and five thousand years of warfare. Back to a particular tent in Anaktuvuk Pass before our modern world rolled in like a bulldozer to bring progress and prosperity.

*   *   *

Noah Ahgook and his wife, Lela, were waiting for us in their tent this particular evening. It was when I first returned to Anaktuvuk Pass with Billie.

Lela, Noah and his old adoptive father, Jesse, along with their four small children, occupied an eight by twelve foot white canvas tent during the summer as did nearly every family in the village.

A few families remained in their one room sod dwellings which were used in the winter. But most of the huts had floors sunk below ground level. In the summer water collects there and they are dark and dank. Soon after spring break-up, when the snow begins to melt, families move out into their summer tents until freeze-up in early October.

*   *   *

Billie and I carefully avoided the dogs, chained a short distance from the front of the tent, and I called "Hello" at the entrance.

I called "Hello" to announce our presence even though we were expected. Everyone in the village knew where we were when I called out "Hello." We paused a moment before we stepped inside.

None rose from where they were seated, but people shifted about for us to find a place on the brush-covered floor.

There were other guests there to meet Billie. She sat, curling her legs beneath her, next to me on the willow branches. After she sat next to me, there were nods and fleeting smiles of acceptance and recognition of a wife who had shared an arctic winter with her mate.

*   *   *

"You like it alone in the mountains when it cold and the sun gone?" Billie was asked.

Her response was that it had been a good experience, not at all depressing as she thought it might be and that she was looking forward to the coming winter.

"You get pretty lonesome for others I think," an older woman said.

Another said, "Now you know how it is for Eskimo early days ago."

Turning to me Lela said, "It good to see you again, Sam. You look younger. Maybe you cut your umik?"

I felt my beard. Everyone laughed.

There was a long pause. Only the sound of children playing outside and dogs barking in the distance were heard while Lela continued scraping the skin on her lap.

*   *   *

The Ahgook's summer tent had a floor of willow branches supplemented by a four by five foot piece of plywood near the entrance. The oblong sheet-iron stove occupied the area to the right of the entrance next to an open shelf cupboard. In it was a can of fruit, a can of condensed milk, a cracker box, a roll of toilet paper and a half loaf of plastic-wrapped commercial bread which had been flown in with us in the mail plane.

On the other side of the entrance was a low table not more than fifteen inches high on which the coffee pot and slices of bread and crackers on a tin plate were placed for our convenience.

The far end of the tent was an alcove, set off by a canvas canopy draped over a rope two feet below the tent's ridge-pole. Blankets, skins and clothing were also hung there. Below them caribou skins and blankets covered two mattresses on the ground where family members lounged and where the four children, grandfather and parents apparently slept.

Fastened to a tent pole were certificates of completion of Head Start courses held early in the summer along with two caribou skin masks made for sale to tourists through traders in Fairbanks.

*   *   *

"See any caribou?"

Noah asked this question which is always the first one asked of someone coming into the village. He had asked it of me earlier but this time it was to open a conversation in which all might join, because to speak of caribou is to speak of life itself.

I said I had seen a band of about ten caribou two day's walk east of Anaktuvuk Pass as we flew in. Also, that among them were calves.

"Pretty good," he said. "Maybe many caribou soon."

Then we talked at length about caribou and how many are needed for the winter. They seemed unbelieving that two or three caribou were all we needed at our home at Koviashuvik, and everyone laughed as if I had made a joke.

When I pointed out that we had no dogs to feed, old Jesse asked something in Eskimo and Lela translated.

"How you pull your sled?"

I pantomimed my role as sled puller and Billie as musher which brought peals of laughter.

Noah said he could carry four carcasses on his sled, but it took seventy-five to a hundred caribou to feed his family and sled dogs for the year.

"You should have some dogs, Sam," he said. "You should have dogs because sometimes when there are no caribou you can eat the dogs."

No one laughed.

As if on cue, the dogs outside the tent began to howl and it was picked up by others until the howling and barking drowned out any conversation and we all sat waiting.

Then the howls ceased as quickly as they began with a few final barks as if a couple were determined to get in the last word like people who always have to get in a last word.

"You should have a dog," Noah repeated. "Maybe three," he said as he got up and added some willow sticks to the coals in the stove and offered us more coffee.

* * *

I was curious to know the villagers' view of the native land claims issue which was before the United States Congress at the time. I wondered what they thought it could mean to them if an agreement was reached to compensate them for their land.

Also, I knew it was not easy to learn what a villager really thinks because it is the custom of these mountain people to consider a person's question carefully and tell him what they believe he wants to hear.

* * *

Once I asked Kakinya if it was very far to a particular lake on the north slope of the range. He heard my question in terms of an obvious wish to visit the lake. He answered my question by saying, "Not far."

He also said it was easy travel. Then he said, like an afterthought, "Maybe you better take plenty supplies."

When I checked a topographic map I discovered the lake to be over seventy air miles away, across four mountain passes and three large rivers. When I pointed this out to Kakinya he said, "It plenty far all right."

* * *

So I approached the native land claims question obliquely by recalling the election day when I was first in the village in 1966. I asked if the log church was still used as a polling place.

* * *

That particular Tuesday, on the twenty-third of August, made a deep impression on me as these Americans at the top of the world cast their ballots.

I recall the soft clucking sounds of the Eskimo language, so new to me then, as Simon Paneak and Jack Ahgook explained voting procedures to the older citizens, often breaking into English with such words as democrat and republican.

The ballot box was a paper bag thumbtacked to the edge of a table and an empty Crayola box received the ballot number stubs.

Nunamiuts came in one or two at a time and voted. They voted then stopped to chat for a while, asking about our hundred mile hike over the passes of the range. Then came the inevitable question.

"See any caribou?"

Always, we were asked about caribou. This usually led to a discussion of other animals such as wolves or moose and where we had seen them.

*   *   *

As for the voting, it was soon evident that there was a large gap between the voters' view and the official view of the election. The official view was how significant an act it was to vote.

When one young Eskimo was asked, as he came in, if he was ready to vote, his reply was, "Same old anak [feces]. It's all anak!"

And then, as if speaking to himself, "No matter who I vote for nothing changes in Anaktuvuk, but give me a piece of paper so I can vote."

Another Eskimo said, "Promises, only promises. Everyone wants to be elected. They say what they will do for the villages but it is just wind."

*   *   *

"The church is still where we vote," Noah said. Then he volunteered what I had not directly asked.

"I think there is too much talk about what we get," he said. "Some people think they will get money because this village is poor but I don't think so. Maybe a new school perhaps. I don't know."

There was a long pause. "It not good to think too much about it."

He blew smoke from his cigarette and watched it stream in front of him.

"We born here," he said. "Eskimo hunt caribou and live in mountains before white men come. This our home."

He looked me directly in the eye and said, "If we get money maybe we cannot hunt any more."

There was another long pause.

"It pretty good to have money though!"

We all laughed long and loud.

*   *   *

Earlier two children had come into the tent and crawled under a caribou skin on the mattress, giggling to each other. They were soon sound asleep.

Billie and I got up and thanked our hosts for the coffee, bread and crackers. We stepped out beneath the snow-topped mountains and made our way around the dogs to crawl into the sleeping bags in our own small tent.

*   *   *

A wolf howled in the distance and the village dogs picked up the cry echoing it back through the pass, a sound familiar to people at this campsite long before Columbus started on his voyage of discovery.

Here they had come in the spring and fall to hunt the caribou migrating over the mountain pass. Here children had been born and here the old who could no longer follow the sled had walked out into the cold to sleep forever. Here they had learned koviashuktok and here the machinery of the modern world was already rolling over the land to bring progress to these Americans of the far north.

*   *   *

As if she read my thoughts, Billie said, "I wonder what will happen to koviashuktok. There seems so little of it left in the world."

> *I never catch myself at any time
> without a perception, and never
> can observe anything but the
> perception.*
>
> DAVID HUME, 1711–1776

18
Phalaropes
A new age

Each summer when we return to Koviashuvik I like to
watch the phalaropes.

Phalaropes are small sandpiper-like birds which many
people do not know exist. They nest in the tundra. They
nest in the tundra at Koviashuvik and spin on the surface of the lake.

I watched a pair fly along the shore. Skimming along
the shore they turned at a sharp angle and dropped to
the glassy surface of the lake, dropped to the glassy surface where sedges grew out into the water.

They drifted light as corks on their own reflections.
On their own reflections their lobed feet spun them
around like tops in one direction and then in the other
as they jabbed for larvae of mosquitos. With needle-like
bills they jabbed for the larvae which rose for air at the
surface of the lake.

*   *   *

Then it happened.

It happened when the flat surface of the water between them swirled and bubbled. The surface roiled and
the larger of the two phalaropes vanished. The little
brown bird vanished as a great northern pike sank slowly
beneath the surface with the phalarope hen in its gullet.

Only wide rolling ripples remained on the surface. The
ripples flattened out into the lake following the male
phalarope's instant flight across the water. Just widen-
ing ripples remained.

Where the birds had been feeding, the surface was
now quiet. It again mirrored back great piles of white
clouds above the surrounding mountains as if nothing
had happened. But the world had changed. Yes, the
world had changed. These northern phalaropes were no
longer a pair. They were different and so was I.

*   *   *

As I thought about this drama, I saw myself as an
explorer.

This is a journey of exploration I am taking and an
explorer can never know what it is he is exploring until
it is explored. This is why I do not know about God,
because I am an explorer.

Many theologians say God is the creator. They assert
a creator. They say there needs to be a creator because
there are things. So, there must be a creator if there is
a creation.

This is impeccable logic. Theologians say it is logical
and natural. But if God is the creator, she or he is logically
and naturally outside its creation. They call it transcen-
dentalism.

Well anyway, if we have an idea that we are created
in the image of God, we will naturally and logically see

ourselves outside the things around us. We will naturally and logically arrogate divinity to ourselves. If we are created in the image of God, the world around us is less entitled to moral or ethical consideration and the environment becomes ours to exploit and the survival unit becomes me and my tribe. This is where we are.

Today, this is where most of us are.

*   *   *

Today, we may eliminate ourselves because we have created God in our image. We think we are created in the image of God but who created whom, I wonder. As an explorer, with a degree in divinity, I wonder because I am an epistemologist.

Mostly because I am a human being, I wonder about phalaropes and if anyone knows answers to ultimate questions.

*   *   *

Anyway, these two small shorebirds probably spent the winter off the coast of Baja, California in Mexico in the company of whales. They had spent the winter in the company of gray whales in the sunshine of Baja before their migration north across open water until they reached the great mud flats where the Yukon river flows into the Bering Sea. There the flock with which they traveled turned inland. They turned to follow the Yukon tributaries north of the Arctic Circle into the Brooks Range.

This pair of phalaropes arrived at Koviashuvik in June along with the terns, sandpipers, yellowlegs, loons and gulls.

They arrived with the same quality of excitement as the other travelers who came seeking a place on the tundra to build a nest. They came seeking a place on the tundra and found just the right spot on the north side of a pebbly spit of land near the water. They found a spot to build their nest like Billie and I found the right spot to build our cabin.

They found a spot where dwarf willow and fireweed grew in scattered clumps. They lined the shallow depression with grass and willow leaves. In it the hen laid four mottled eggs.

        *   *   *

Among phalaropes the male takes charge of the nest as soon as the eggs are laid.

For the next eighteen days the cock sat on the nest until the chicks cracked their shells and emerged as little puffs, little balls of fluff, no larger than the tuft on a stem of tundra cotton grass.

Within two weeks, the downy chicks were clothed with feathers and could fly with their parents. They could fly with their parents and spin themselves around on the lake surface as they jabbed for insects in the shallows along the shore.

        *   *   *

Now, late in July, the nesting is done.

The young have been taught to hide from predators, taught to find food and to know the phalarope rules of life and death. Just as we have rules of life and death, phalaropes have rules. Even if they cannot think about them, they have premises. They have premises developed through thousands of years that have helped them survive.

As long as things do not change too much their premises work. They pass them on to their young. They pass them on before they fly south with the flock along the Yukon.

This year, only one of the parents will join the flock across the open water of the Pacific to meet the whales off the coast of Baja. Only one.

*   *   *

Life pays little attention to tragedy in the wilderness of the Brooks Range because tragedy depends upon the point of view. Yes it does.

For the great northern pike, with a phalarope digesting in its stomach, it has been a good day.

*   *   *

Now listen to this.

We know what we know because we have basic beliefs which are based on how we know what we know.

The study of how we know what we know is called epistemology. How we know what we know is important today. It is important because today reality is not what we once observed it to be. The world, as we once perceived it to be flat, is now round. Because we changed our epistemological premises, it is round. It was round before we changed our epistemological premises but we could not perceive it as round until we corrected our epistemology.

*   *   *

Anyway, there comes a time when the world as we have perceived it no longer makes sense. Only when it no longer makes sense as we once perceived it is it possible to consider different ideas and perceptions.

To become aware that reality is not what we observed it to be is uncomfortable. Yes it is.

Throughout human history most people have been able to avoid thinking and so we have not changed most of our premises even though we know they no longer fit.

We hold on to epistemological premises that we had better change or our survival is uncertain. In a technological world our survival is uncertain and we know it.

*   *   *

Well, the time has come when it is possible to consider different ideas and perceptions. The time has come, but there is no guarantee that new ideas or perceptions will necessarily be an improvement over the old. There is no guarantee.

If reality does not mean what we once thought it did, there is no guarantee that new ideas and perceptions will be an improvement but I hope so.

*   *   *

It has been said that nature cares for the species and sacrifices the individual. That the race, the tribe, the state, the nation come first has been a premise as old as civilization. That nature cares for the species and sacrifices the individual is a perception not only assumed in nature but in government and the military and all the institutions we have created.

Yes, it has been one of our basic perceptions that nature cares for the species and sacrifices the individual. Nature lavishes its care on the resources of reproduction and exhausts the energy of the parent in the launching of the child. The child in time will be exhausted for the sake of its child and when it is done the phalarope or person may live on as something we cherish but nature merely tolerates.

*   *   *

Nature cares for nothing. Only humans have care. Nature only has necessity.

Yes, nature only has necessity. A species or race has no individual consciousness. Neither has an institution, state or nation. The only thing that can care is an individual.

What if, in the last resort, it is the individual that must make up for the mortality of the species? I wonder if it is the individual. Not the race. It may be that in the last resort it is the individual. Not the group but the individual.

*   *   *

Now consider this.

The individual in her or his reproductive capacity sends off a new generation as a pledge to the future. Instead of exhausting themselves, as persons they are matured. They mature themselves in assuming a mental as well as physical responsibility for the ongoing stream of life. This is what it means to be a person. To be a person means living for something more than self. It is a faith in adventure.

*   *   *

People talk a great deal about faith today. They talk about the importance of having faith.

It is yesterday in which they have faith. Yes, it is in yesterday, not in today or tomorrow. I find it strange that revelation belongs to yesterdays. The gods have always come to earth to take human form in the long ago, never now. No never now.

We are supported by structures of the past to which we have become accustomed while a new age coming into being rises all around us.

We are anachronisms. Most of us are anachronisms, belonging in another age yet living in this one.

Adventure, whether physical or mental, implies breaking into unpenetrated ground, venturing beyond the boundary of normal aptitude, extending oneself to the limit of capacity, courageously facing peril. Life without the chance for such exertions would be a dreary game, scarcely bearable in its horrible banality.

ROBERT MARSHALL, 1901–1939

19
Faith of Adventure
The myths by which we live

Of all the forms of life which nature has produced we are the strangest and most complex. Human beings are the strangest. Yes we are.

*   *   *

We are not as strange and complex in our physical structure. Our hearts and our lungs and blood are much like the wolf and caribou. When a grizzly bear is skinned it looks so much like a human being that some tribes of Indians and Eskimos refer to bears as people. They call animals people of another tribe and so do I.

Yes, I think all animals are people of different tribes because they are.

*   *   *

Anyway, it is not so much our physical structure as it is our inner life. It is the inner life above all else. It is the inner life that is the distinguishing characteristic of the human species.

* * *

All forms of life pursue activity which can become quite complicated. Especially higher forms of life we call animals pursue courses of activity which become complex. The activity can become very complicated but it appears that this activity is the means to a fixed end. Always it appears to be a means toward a fixed and obvious end called survival.

Everything animals do seems aimed at the one objective of survival. Wherever they are they struggle for food and shelter. They struggle to propagate the species. They struggle to protect their own life and that of their young.

Yes, they struggle to survive. All animals struggle to survive but a concern with values as we know them plays little or no part in the conduct of their lives.

* * *

I watched a swarm of bees build a hive in the rocky sandstone cleft of a canyon wall and it was a masterpiece. It was a masterpiece of engineering and form.

It was a masterpiece of ingenuity and beauty but I never saw a single bee stand off to admire its handiwork. Bees do not try to understand the way in which the hive came into being. At least I do not think so, or the purpose for which it was created.

I know of no animals except people who are concerned with values and even here I wonder about people. At least about some people.

* * *

Now consider this.

We are cursed or blessed with self-consciousness. In the Garden of Eden story, Adam and Eve were cursed when they ate fruit from the tree of knowledge. In the

Hebrew-Christian-Muslim myth, humans were cursed when their eyes were opened and they became like gods.

In Hinduism and Buddhism, the curse is the wheel of self-consciousness, the wheel of Karma, from which we would escape if we could.

If we believe what we have been told, most of us would cease to be human. We would choose to be bees. Yes, I think we would even if I do not like the idea. If people believe what they say they do, they would choose not to be human.

*　　*　　*

As I said, we are cursed or blessed with a burning desire to understand, with an ability to go beyond what the past has given us to try to create something new and finer. We seem to be driven by a relentless urge which will not let us be content merely to promote our bodily survival and perpetuate our species.

*　　*　　*

When we have achieved that level of existence in which our physical wants are more or less satisfied, and our future seems relatively secure, it is then we are most plagued by the desire to understand. It is then we most want to know and go beyond what we have achieved to something that is higher.

Here is the beginning of the philosophical and religious quest of any person in any time by whatever name we call it. This intense longing to uncover some meaning beyond mere survival. This desire to fathom the mysteries of the universe and discern the reason for existence.

*　　*　　*

I remember when I killed our first caribou. It was a clean shot in the neck and I was delighted that we had winter meat.

For Billie it was a traumatic experience. I felt it was a traumatic experience for Billie, who until then had always had her meat come plastic-wrapped or weighed out by a butcher in the meat market.

She helped me skin and quarter the handsome buck while I talked. Because I was concerned for her I talked.

I pointed out that all food means the death of some plant or animal but it is seldom personal in the evasive suburban world. However, here we were intimately involved with survival.

*   *   *

After supper, survival seemed less important with the caribou tongue boiling in a pot on the Yukon stove filling the cabin with fragrance.

I wonder how many cattle, hogs, sheep and chickens passed through slaughter houses that day while I was prying into the mystery of life and death. While I was reaching under the rib cage beyond the great heart now still, pulling tissues from his wind-pipe to remove the lungs. Breath and beating heart no longer.

That caribou became part of our blood and bones. His skin padded our spruce pole bed and we survived our first winter.

But there is something more. Yes, I still see him standing wild before the rifle kicked. There he still stands, wild and free, and here he is in these ink marks on this paper.

*   *   *

This desire to fathom the mysteries of the universe and discern the reason for existence is not a matter of choice. I am convinced it is not a matter of choice. By our very nature we are impelled to reflect on life and the universe.

We are possessed with an insatiable nagging curiosity. At least some of us are possessed with an insatiable curiosity that demands to explore why we exist and why we are alive and what the world in which we live is really like. It is a faith of adventure that demands to explore and discover or create explanations for the significance of all things.

*   *   *

It was the first of October. We had sourdough pancakes and caribou ribs for breakfast.

The morning was glittering white with new snow and ten degrees above zero while I sharpened the adz on a stump in the sunshine. I sharpened the eight-inch adz with a file in the sparkling sunshine while I thought about the willows I was going to cut to clear a trail before winter. There is much to be learned from willows.

*   *   *

Alders and willows, from pencil size to an inch in diameter are not easy to cut, especially willows. Willows are not easy to cut because the wood is so limber and the wands bend in such a manner that the edge of the tool does not catch but only slides along the stem scraping off the bark. Then the willow flies up. It flies up whipping the trail-maker in the face. No matter what tool is used the willow wands fly up whipping the trail-maker as if in defiance.

*   *   *

There is something strong and tenacious about these pioneer plants which fill in where tundra and spruce trees have been disturbed by people or fires. They are good ptarmigan and moose forage which is in their favor. But to hike through them or attempt to cut them to make a trail is frustrating. It is frustrating because of their resiliency. It is their resiliency which gives them their quality of strength and tenacity. It is as if ancient willows had foreseen the challenge of an adz in their future and developed a resiliency to meet it.

It is this very resiliency which is so maddening to the

person trying to deal with them. Some people also seem to have this same resiliency developed through generations of selection.

*   *   *

Anyway, we not only want to be alive, at least most people want to be alive and maintain their lives, but people yearn to know why they are alive and what is the purpose of living.

Even those who say there is no purpose, or that to question is meaningless, are not willing to accept things as they are. No, they are not willing to accept things in society or themselves or the world around them but are impelled to explain, to question, to change, to improve.

From the earliest recorded times we seem to have been plagued by ever-recurring questions to which we feel we must find or create answers.

*   *   *

In one sense our quest today, our exploration and venture, is the same as that with which people in every age have wrestled.

No matter what forms myths or scientific postulates have taken, a way has never been found to answer with any certainty the questions with which, by our very nature, we are concerned. No way has been found, yet we all answer these questions. Yes, we all give answers to these questions whether consciously or not.

Whether by intention or default we give answers, and our answers determine the kind of life we lead. Our answers determine the satisfactions and contributions made to life and the world community in which we live.

We all give answers in every action we take. Our understanding of life and our attitude toward the universe points to the myths by which we live. We live our real beliefs in these answers. In these myths we live our real beliefs while professing others.

Even though we may not think of them as myths they are, because a myth articulates what we wish to be true. It may not be reality. A myth is not reality. It is what we wish and it tells us how to act.

*   *   *

Here are the myths by which we live.

Our mythology says there is a cosmos, a coherent universe that can be known, that there is order every-where and human beings are creatures who can know it. Because the universe is coherent, human beings can know it.

Our mythology says the universe exists as our home, a home in which human beings may prosper whether or not anything else does. The goodness of the universe exists as a home for human beings and each person possesses inherent value. Each person possesses a sanc-tity and the capability to act rightly.

Our mythology says human dignity is confirmed in individual freedom. In individual freedom human dignity is confirmed and individual freedom is an ultimate value.

*   *   *

Well, in the past, old premises worked. The myths by which we lived seemed to confirm themselves. But now we are in a time of change and old patterns are questioned.

No longer do we know if the universe is knowable, or if humans are rational. We do not know if there is everywhere a conformity to laws, or that the universe will provide for us, or if human life is sacred, or if freedom is real or good. We do not know.

These are the past myths by which we lived. We have lived by these myths but we could not see them as myths. Now we can.

Now that we can it is not comfortable. No, it is not comfortable when all contemporary myths are suspect.

Because we are myth makers and our myths are suspect it is not comfortable.

*   *   *

So here we are at a time in our journey when the myths by which we have lived and the premises we have held may no longer fit.

It is a time for faith in adventure. It is a time to become explorers again in a new age rising all about us. It is a time for exploration, a renewed faith.

*   *   *

It is time to pioneer myths on more basic foundations.

Even though we know these more basic myths will be no more provable than those of the past, they will be our foundation as we move ahead into the great uncertainty beyond the now.

We know we go with courage for we are survivors and that has taught us the art of courage.

We have beauty. Yes, on every side of darkness and despair we see, hear, feel, know and are gladdened by the glory of the world in the pattern which connects us with this sacred place, this earth which is our home.

The Eskimo calls it koviashuktok.

Whatever its name, we know that life is a great and miraculous gift to be honored and treasured. We shall honor and treasure it because we have each other to share the future, whatever the unknowns.

Finally, each of us arrives east of the sun and west of the moon with a faith which is not blind belief in what may be, but life in spite of consequences, a faith in our need to affirm the adventure of this sacred journey we all share.

Postscript

In the summer of 1987 Billie had an operation for breast cancer followed with a trial chemotherapy treatment. By Thanksgiving time she felt the quality of her life had so deteriorated that keeping alive was too great a burden.

*   *   *

She wanted to die in the northern wilderness at Koviashuvik but was so weak she was unable to make the trip from the central Arizona mountains.

So on December 7, a day she picked because it was Pearl Harbor Day and "It might be the beginning of world peace as Gorbachev of the Soviet Union is visiting the President of the United States," Billie delivered herself from the trauma and indignity of a lingering death and died in my arms.

*   *   *

At the close of her journal of our life in the Alaskan wilderness she had added the following postscript: "If the world of my dailiness beyond the Arctic Circle sings to you, do not make the mistake of coming to the arctic wilderness in hope of finding the same song. You must discover your own, not mine. You must discover your own Koviashuvik."

When summer arrived I scattered her ashes as she requested, "On the knoll where the cranberries at Koviashuvik grow the thickest and finest."

Sam Wright
September 13, 1988